Beauty in the Word

To my family

STRATFORD CALDECOTT

Beauty in the Word

*Rethinking the
Foundations of Education*

Angelico Press

First published in the USA
by Angelico Press
© Stratford Caldecott 2012
Foreword © Anthony Esolen 2012

For information, address:
Angelico Press, 4619 Slayden Rd., NE
Tacoma, WA 98422
www.angelicopress.com

Library of Congress Cataloging-in-Publication Data

Caldecott, Stratford.
Beauty in the word: rethinking the foundations of education /
Stratford Caldecott.—1st ed.

p. cm.

Includes bibliographical references and index.
ISBN 978-1-62138-004-7 (pbk: alk. paper)
1. Education—Philosophy. 2. Education, Humanistic—Great Britain.
3. Language arts—Great Britain. 4. Catholic Schools—Great Britain.
I. Title.
LB14.7.C345 2012
370.01—dc2   2012013698

Cover Image: Fra Angelico,
The Sermon on the Mount, c. 1440
Cover Design: Cristy Deming

CONTENTS

Acknowledgments

THIS BOOK would not have happened but for another that I published under the title *Beauty for Truth's Sake* (Brazos, 2009). That was a study of the classical 'Quadrivium'—the four mathematical or cosmological arts that once formed an essential part of a liberal education, preparing the student for the study of philosophy and theology. My book started with an interest in the symbolic and aesthetic qualities of numbers and shapes (I hasten to add unaccompanied by any expertise in mathematics or geometry), and became a kind of plea or even a manifesto for the reintegration in education of the arts and sciences. It was well received, and I was approached to write a sequel that would deal with the three preparatory arts, the 'Trivium' or liberal arts of language. That project turned into the present book, which might have been subtitled 'Why the Trivium is Far from Trivial.' Together the two books are intended to draw inspiration from the seven liberal arts for the purpose of rethinking the foundations of Catholic education in our own time. They are, I should stress, a work in progress.

I must therefore particularly thank Fr Dominic O'Connor and his brother Greg O'Connor for commissioning this book as part of their broader UK-based project intended to produce resources for education and the 'new evangelization.' Without them it would simply not have been written. I want to thank also my new publishers, John Riess and James Wetmore, whose enthusiasm and encouragement at just the right time meant and continues to mean a great deal to me. Many others have given useful feedback on the book at different stages, including Jim Maroosis, Matthew Milliner, Fr Dominic O'Connor, Roy Peachey, Margaret Atkins, and Carol Bowling—and of course those who read the book for the publisher, including Fr Aidan Nichols OP, Fr James V. Schall SJ, and Dr Cyrus P. Olsen III, and especially the author of the Foreword, Anthony Esolen.

The reader is urged to refer to the author's website for further discussion of the philosophy and reform of education at *http://beauty-in-education.blogspot.com*, including practical aspects which have only been touched on in this volume. As mentioned, this book is part of a wider, ongoing project, and I am excited at the prospect of helping to develop over the next few years, if God permits and with the assistance of teachers and parents on both sides of the Atlantic, other books and supporting materials for homes, schools, and parishes.

STRATFORD CALDECOTT

Foreword

Anthony Esolen

I SHOULD LIKE to introduce Stratford Caldecott's wonderful and much needed book with an anecdote, followed by a brief survey of the wasteland. A few years ago I was at a book sale, at a local library in Canada. I hadn't found anything I liked, so a young girl came up to me to ask if she could help. She was a worker at the library, and was about to enter the most esteemed college in eastern Canada. 'What are you interested in?' she asked.

That was a hard question for me to answer, since we didn't really speak the same language. I could have said, 'Perceptive works in philosophy and theology,' or 'Great European novels,' but I don't think that would have advanced the conversation. I finally said that I was a college professor, and when she asked me what I taught, I mentioned Dante and the *Divine Comedy.*

'I don't mean any disrespect for your favorite author,' she said, smiling, 'but I've never heard of him.'

I could multiply this anecdote many times over. From what my freshmen now tell me, public schools in the United States have virtually abandoned the study of literature written before 1900, and their neglect of poetry in general is more thoroughgoing still. Some few of them have read perhaps a sonnet by John Donne, typically 'Death, Be Not Proud,' or a piece of the prologue of Chaucer's *Canterbury Tales.* Sometimes there's a play by Shakespeare, a *Macbeth* or *Romeo and Juliet,* taught, of course, without any reference to the Christian faith that formed the world wherein Shakespeare and his audience found their home. It's not as if their place were taken by the quintessentially American mythographers and poets. Hawthorne rarely makes it into the room; Melville and Longfellow more rarely still. *Huckleberry Finn* has fallen victim to political sensitivities, despite Mark

Twain's heroic championing of the goodness and wisdom of the slave, Jim. Robert Frost is forgotten, even in New England. James Fenimore Cooper is forgotten, even in New York. I am informed by my British colleagues that if I entertain some quaint notion that Wordsworth and Coleridge are remembered in England, I am seriously mistaken.

And yet somehow that neglect isn't the worst of it. When I find out what they do read, I'm struck by what can only be described as a perverse refusal to assign literature of any real beauty. There are the political novels, the exploration of what is ugly and tawdry in the modern world, and books assigned to 'open' the mind by exposing it to a favorite perversion, with a dash of obscenity or pornography to season the dish. The same faults may be found in the forgetting of history, and the turn towards the ephemera of current events; or in the neglect of the logic of language, grammar, for the benefit of self-expression, preferably of the daintily crude variety. I am tempted to conclude that there are only two things wrong with our schools: what they don't teach our children, and what they do.

That is where the criticism of our schools usually begins and ends. I don't wish to deny the validity of that criticism; it is scandalous that children in England will not know who Thomas Becket was, or that children in America will not know what happened at Yorktown. But as Stratford Caldecott so beautifully shows in his much-needed work, we suffer the consequences of a more fundamental error still. We do not know what or how to teach children, because we do not know what a child is, and we do not know what a child is, because we do not know what man is—and Him from whom and for whom man is.

How decisive for the Christian educator, or for any educator of good will, is the revelation that man is made in the image and likeness of the three-Personed God? That is like asking what difference it will make to us if we keep in mind that a human being is made not for the processing of data, but for wisdom; not for the utilitarian satisfaction of appetite, but for love; not for the domination of nature, but for participation in it; not for the autonomy of an isolated self, but for communion. It is no accident that Caldecott has structured his plan for a true education

4

upon the three ways of the Trivium, which themselves reflect the three primary axes of being, revealed by God: of knowing, that is to say giving; of being known, that is to say receiving; and of the loving gift. As Dante puts it:

> O Light that dwell within Thyself alone,
> who alone know Thyself, are known, and smile
> with Love upon the Knowing and the Known!

If we did keep these things in mind, I doubt very much that we would trammel children up in great warehouses, built for the efficient delivery of services of quite dubious value. But more than that, we would desire to bring children into the garden of created being, and thought, and expression. Caldecott reminds us that for the medieval schoolmen, as for Plato, education was essentially musical, an education in the cosmos or lovely order that surrounds us and bears us up. Thus when we teach our youngest children by means of rhymes and songs, we do so not merely because rhymes and songs are actually effective mnemonic devices. We do so because we wish to form their souls by memory: we wish to bring them up as rememberers, as persons, born, as Caldecott points out, in certain localities, among certain people, who bear a certain history, and who claim our love and loyalty.

The memory, too, gives the child both the strength and the armor he needs for what comes next, and that is thought itself—strength to search for truth, and armor against easy and plausible falsehoods. I often hear well-meaning people say that they do not teach children *what* to think, but *how* to think. What they mean is that they reward genuine thought, rather than thoughtless repetition of what the teacher has said. Yet this way of looking at things is wholly inadequate, because it does not originate in truth, nor does it have truth as its ardent aim. Consider an analogy. Suppose an art teacher should say, 'I do not teach my students what to draw, but how to draw.' Yet one cannot proceed one step in drawing without the what. The what and the how are inextricably bound. That is the case too for the relationship between memory and thought. Yes, there are rules of logic, which Caldecott, wise Socratic as he is, duly emphasizes. But he knows also that reason itself is far more than the nominally correct use of deductive rules. It involves the whole mind and its apprehension of the *what* outside: grass, and dogs, and rivers, and justice, and love. So the study of how to think is also a deepening of one's first memories, or one's first encounters with truth. Or we might put it another way, and say that the Son reveals to us the Father, and that the Son does only what He sees the Father do.

Yet what good would all this be to us, if we were to put the lamp under a bushel basket, or retire, guru-like, into the mountains, in calm separation from the lot of our fellow men? Thus Caldecott completes his art of education with Speaking: with the Spirit. He recalls for us the *ruah* or the breath of God, stirring upon the waters of creation; it is that same breath that inspired, literally in-breathed, the apostles at Pentecost. Only then could these very ordinary men go forth, in courage, to preach the good news of Jesus Christ. The Lord who made the mute to speak, made the disciples to preach. The art of rhetoric, the third course of the Trivium, is not for political gain, as the Sophists of ancient Greece once boasted that they could teach young men to sway the democratic assemblies whichever way they would. It is for the attractive showing of truth: it wins for truth with eloquence, and beauty, and the love-born wish to bring others into communion with those who see that truth.

This is an education in reality—the reality of the world, and of persons. It involves, in memory, the child's appropriation of realities; in thinking, the older child's exploration of those realities; in speaking, the youth's sharing of those realities with others, in a community. It is an education that penetrates the heart and the mind with light. After so long a journey into the depths of the drab and the dispirited, it is as if we were beckoned by this wise and happy man to ascend with him at last, and see, once more, the stars.

Introduction

The Need for Foundations

WE LIVE at a time when many parents are trying to take back control of schools and schooling from politicians and bureaucrats who have lost their trust. In Britain, some politicians are willing to give it back to them. New opportunities for school reform, and the creation of Academy schools and Free schools, comparable to American Charter schools, make it possible again to think radically about education. In order to do that, we must make an effort to understand the elements and assumptions that make a good education possible.

In the United States, the public school system has long been a cultural disaster. Hope lies largely with the homeschooling movement, and with attempts to revive classical education, both at home and in a growing number of schools and small liberal arts colleges. But there is a need to look more closely at the philosophy that underlies these movements.

Ideas have consequences.[1] They shape our society, our economy, our very lives. The gravest threat our civilization faces is in fact not ecological but philosophical. It is the widespread belief that there is no objective truth and no 'true' way of considering the world and its history, only a plurality of subjective points of view, each point of view being of equal value and deserving equal respect. Of course, there are also limits to the views that can be given respect, and these limits are supposed to exclude any perspective that might give rise to violent behavior (such as Nazism or Islamism). Ironically, since our society has given up the notion of objective truth, these undesirable opinions cannot be engaged rationally. Instead they must simply be suppressed, with more or

---

1 This is the title of a well-known book by Richard Weaver that has had a great influence on the conservative movement in America.

less subtle violence—violence that often feeds the grievances of the suppressed community.

This book asserts that we need truth. We need a philosophy that can guide us as we found new schools, or enrich and improve existing schools, or attempt to design a curriculum for teaching our children at home. Our curricula have become fragmented and incoherent because we have lost any sense of how all knowledge fits together. Students graduate with some knowledge of, say, the Tudors or the Second World War, Romantic poetry or astrophysics, without any awareness of other historical periods or the classical origins of our civilization. It is as though we were attempting to construct the top floor of a building without bothering with the lower floors or foundations. And most importantly of all, if education is to be effective it needs to be based on knowledge about the nature and purpose of human life—a true, or at least adequate, 'anthropology.' This knowledge is what the modern relativist thinks impossible. But religious believers hold that the truth has been revealed, even if our grasp of it remains limited and unreliable. I write from within the Catholic tradition, according to which Jesus Christ reveals us to ourselves (to borrow an expression from Vatican II) and shows us that love is the true meaning of the world.

In love we see the beauty that moves the sun and stars, the beauty that draws together all the sciences and arts of man into a whole vision of reality. This is the beauty of Wisdom, 'more moving than any motion,' the 'brightness of the everlasting light.'[2] It is the love of Wisdom that inspires a Catholic philosophy of education.

An Education in Freedom

The kind of education we want is one that fits us to know the truth that will set us free. 'All human beings by nature stretch themselves out toward knowing,' said Aristotle.[3] All human beings desire to know the truth, to know reality. There are many

2 Wisdom 7:24–6, KJV. See Endnote 8 for more about Wisdom.
3 The first line of the Metaphysics, from *Aristotle's Metaphysics*.

who wish to deceive others, but few who want to be deceived (and therefore enslaved).

Ideally, Catholicism fulfils and brings to perfection the natural educational process, which is the transmission in creative freedom of a cultural tradition to our children. Whether Catholic or not, the particular educational tradition to which the readers of this book will be assumed to belong is that of European civilization. This is associated with what have been termed the 'liberal arts.' The liberal arts are a golden thread that comes from the Greeks, from Pythagoras and his successors both Islamic and Christian, especially St Augustine; a thread that weaves its way through the history of our civilization. These arts were intended for the cultivation of freedom and the raising of our humanity to its highest possible level.

In ancient times, the liberal arts were reserved for an elite—an elite of men, that is, excluding women, and of free men only, excluding slaves. Today, in democratic societies, all men and women participate together in ruling our society, even if only by electing representatives to do so, and the education that used to be reserved to aristocrats is now a necessary qualification for everyone. If we are all to rule, we all need to become wise, and the key to wisdom is to understand the unity or interrelationship of all human knowledge, which is where the liberal arts come in.

The liberal arts were sevenfold, and the first three, the *Trivium* ('place where three roads meet'), on which this book is focused, were about the use of *verbal symbols* to think and communicate. These arts consisted in Grammar, Dialectic (also called Logic), and Rhetoric. According to Hugh of Saint Victor, summarizing this tradition in the high Middle Ages, 'Grammar is the knowledge of how to speak without error; dialectic is clear-sighted argument which separates the true from the false; rhetoric is the discipline of persuading to every suitable thing.'[4] The second group, the 'meeting of four ways' or *Quadrivium*, was about the use of mathematical symbols in Arithmetic, Geometry, Music, and Astronomy.[5]

---

4 *The* Didascalicon *of Hugh of Saint Victor*, 82.
5 See Endnote 1 for a summary of the history of the liberal arts.

The first three, the arts of language, have been neglected in recent years in our thinking about education and the core curriculum. In this book I am interested less in the historical realization of this ideal in the Middle Ages—which was always far from perfect—than in the inspiration that lay behind it. I want to derive inspiration from the liberal arts for our present. That is the reason you will find the chapter on Grammar headed 'Remembering,' the one on Dialectic headed 'Thinking,' and the one on Rhetoric headed 'Speaking.' I wanted to emphasize the fact that we are discussing the fundamental skills of humanity itself. So under 'Remembering' I reflect on the birth of language and how Being reveals itself in speech. Under 'Thinking' I am concerned more precisely with the use of language to reveal *what is true* and what is not, and the question of how we know which is which. Under 'Speaking' I look at how we *communicate* what we know to others within a moral community of free persons.

We need also to pay some attention to the visual and other arts, not to mention history and the study of nature, which are often overlooked in the 'Great Books' approach to Classical Education but which certainly belong integrally to a rounded curriculum. The seven liberal arts were in any case never intended to constitute the whole of education. They were embedded in a broader tradition of *paideia* or human formation, which included 'gymnastics' for the education of the body and 'music' for the education of the soul (terms that have changed and narrowed in meaning over the centuries). The arts were intended to prepare the ground for the attainment of wisdom and truth in philosophy and theology. The full range of subjects studied would include practical skills associated with the arts and crafts (*techne*) through to the highest reaches of wisdom (*sophia*). Today, those skills and associated abilities would include a facility with machines and computers. The ability to think critically and for oneself is a part of this tradition, but not in separation from the moral virtues. Conceptual and dialectical thought is not the highest activity of man, but gives way before contemplation and the development of the spirit through love.

I have already written in *Beauty for Truth's Sake* about the 'disenchantment' of the world that took place in modern times. We have *educated ourselves to believe* that meaning and purpose, if they exist at all, are not given by a Creator or divine source but are invented and imposed upon the world by man. If, as a society, we agree on certain values it must be because we have negotiated such agreement through the procedures of Market or State, not because we have submitted ourselves to an objective truth. I wrote in that book of the need to recover a 'poetic' way of knowing the meaning of things by reforging the connection between self and world. The self is not a separate substance, condemned only to observe the world from a distance, but can understand it from the inside by a kind of imaginative sympathy, learning to read (no doubt at first naively) the language of nature.

But what kind of education would enable a child to progress in the rational understanding of the world without losing his poetic and artistic appreciation of it? This is what I am searching for in the present book. Inadequate though my answers may be, I know the questions are valid. Rationality and poetry, science and art, need not be opposed. After all, we owe scientific breakthroughs as much to great acts of imagination as to feats of observation or calculation (one thinks of Einstein trying to picture running alongside a beam of light, or comparing in his mind's eye the experience of being in a falling lift or elevator with that of floating freely in space, on the basis of which he developed the special and general theories of relativity). It must be possible to use this intrinsic connection between reason and imagination to overcome the alienation between the humanities and sciences.

The central idea of the present book is very simple. It is that education is not primarily about the acquisition of information. It is not even about the acquisition of 'skills' in the conventional sense, to equip us for particular roles in society. It is about how we become more human (and therefore more free, in the truest sense of that word). This is a broader and a deeper question, but no less practical. Too often we have not been educating our humanity. We have been educating ourselves for *doing* rather than for *being*. We live in an excessively activist civilization, in which contemplation and interiority are often despised and suppressed in favor of mere action and reaction. The task before us is not only to renew the foundations of education, but to rediscover our own relationship to Being (the secret of childhood), and our place in a cosmos that is *beautiful in the Word*.

The Specific Mission of a Catholic School

It will be obvious that this book is addressed partly, though not exclusively, to Roman Catholics. In an address to the Bishops of the United Kingdom during his visit in September 2010, as in many other speeches in other Western countries, Benedict XVI reiterated the Church's call for a New Evangelization, meaning the 'urgent need to proclaim the Gospel afresh in a highly secularized environment.' This has implications for education, for, as the Church often repeats, a *Catholic school is by its nature a place of evangelization*. 'The mission of the Church is to evangelize, for the interior transformation and the renewal of humanity. For young people, the school is one of the ways for this evangelization to take place.'[6]

Such remarks might cause trepidation, in a world perceived as full of rampaging religious fanatics. Are our schools to be training grounds for holy warriors? Not at all. The 'New Evangelization' is not about making converts at the point of the sword. In an interview given to journalists on his way to Scotland in September 2010, Pope Benedict XVI stressed that the duty to evangelize did not even mean that we must be particularly concerned with numbers, or with struggling to act in such a way that more people will convert. For:

> One might say that a church which seeks above all to be attractive would already be on the wrong path, because the Church does not work for herself, does not work to increase

---

6 Congregation for Catholic Education, *The Religious Dimension of Education in a Catholic School*, 33, 66. A subsequent document by the Congregation, 'The Catholic School on the Threshold of the Third Millennium' (1997), reiterated this point in the light of the growing 'crisis of values which, in highly developed societies in particular, assumes the form, often exalted by the media, of subjectivism, moral relativism and nihilism' (section 1). All the Congregation's documents are freely available at *www.vatican.va* (the Vatican website).

her numbers so as to have more power. The Church is at the service of Another; she does not serve herself, seeking to be a strong body, but strives to make the Gospel of Jesus Christ accessible, the great truths, the great powers of love and of reconciliation that appeared in this figure and that come always from the presence of Jesus Christ. In this sense, the Church does not seek to be attractive, but rather to make herself transparent for Jesus Christ. And in the measure in which the Church is not for herself, as a strong and powerful body in the world that wishes to have power, but simply is herself the voice of Another, she becomes truly transparent to the great figure of Jesus Christ and the great truths that he has brought to humanity, the power of love; it is then when the Church is heard and accepted. She should not consider herself, but assist in considering the Other, and should herself see and speak of the Other and for the Other.[7]

The mission to evangelize does not imply, either, that we who happen to be Catholics believe ourselves to be saved by virtue of our membership in the Church, while all others are destined for hellfire unless they repent and join us. Such misconceptions have been laid to rest by the Second Vatican Council and the *Catechism of the Catholic Church*. Others may not be saved by their own religions; but they can be saved *within* them, by virtue of the grace of Christ that is made available to everyone who does not deliberately reject it—the 'true light that enlightens every man' (John 1:9). Nevertheless, as a believer, I want to share the fullness of God's self-revelation with everyone. In that sense I do want to make converts, not for the sake of numbers, but to draw others towards Christ in the Church. I should like everyone to have the benefit of God's intimate presence in the sacraments.[8] Evangelization is part of the mission of a Catholic, and part of the mission

---

7 Interview with journalists during Apostolic Visit to the United Kingdom, 16 September 2010, translation from *www.vatican.va* (slightly edited).

8 Even if, to our shame, having this benefit has not made us noticeably better than our neighbors. Perhaps we should admit the fact that the closer we come to Christ, or he to us (and in the Eucharist he comes as close as he can),

of a Catholic school—provided we understand that we must constantly evangelize ourselves first, turning ourselves back to the true service of Christ.

In fact, before his election as Pope, in 2000, Cardinal Ratzinger gave a wonderful discourse on the principles and methods of the New Evangelization to catechists and religion teachers.[9] In it he began: 'Our life is an open question, an incomplete project, still to be brought to fruition and realized. Each man's fundamental question is: How will this be realized—becoming man? How does one learn the art of living? Which is the path toward happiness?' And he continued: 'To evangelize means: to show this path—to teach the art of living. . . . But this art is not the object of a science—this art can only be communicated by [one] who has life—he who is the Gospel personified.'

The news of the Incarnation is not some piece of information that, once communicated, can be filed away, and which changes nothing. If true, it changes everything. It reveals the meaning and purpose of life, and this releases the floodgates of human creativity. And yet the beginning and end of the Christian life is not evangelization but love, as Benedict XVI taught in his first encyclical, *Deus Caritas Est*. Love is the beginning and end of education, because love is the way we become more human. This is why a 'Catholic identity' poses no threat to human freedom, and why on the contrary it offers greater possibilities for human flourishing even to non-believers.

The 'Catholicism' in a Catholic school cannot simply be added on to an existing curriculum or atmosphere. Precisely because a

---

the more graces we may obtain, but also the more dangers and temptations beset us—including the temptation to self-righteousness, which is a form of pride, the sin of sins. We can become saints; but we may also become veritable devils if we are not extremely careful. There is no way back. Once embarked on the narrow way to God's house, we cannot turn or wander off the track as we could when we lived in the pleasant meadows of ignorance. If that sounds harsh and difficult, it is also exciting and consoling. For God is close, and that is what creates both the danger and the promise. 'He who conquers shall not be hurt by the second death' (Rev. 2:11).

9 12 December 2000, *www.ewtn.com/new_evangelization/Ratzinger.htm* (accessed 30 July 2011).

religious faith affects everything, even changing the way we view the cosmos, it cannot be compartmentalized. (This is why faith seems so dangerous to some non-believers.) Revelation subtly alters the way every subject is taught as well as the relationships between them. What is revealed connects them severally and together to our own destiny, to the desire of our hearts for union with infinite truth. At that point, *everything* becomes interesting. There are no 'boring' subjects—nothing can be ugly or pointless unless we make it so, turning our backs on the Giver of Being.

The Heart of the Book

So what is this book trying to say, and why are the chapters on Grammar, Dialectic, and Rhetoric at its heart? To those who have been cut off and feel some sense of alienation from the great tradition and community of our civilization, the book is trying to say:

Be!

(Grammar)

Think!   **Speak!**

(Dialectic)   (Rhetoric)

The Trinitarian structure is intentional. It may help to keep it in mind as you progress through the book. The following notes on this structure will probably make more sense when you reach the end.

An education for freedom (a 'liberal' education) is underpinned by a Trinitarian theology as follows.

In order to *Be* we must remember our origin and end, the grammar of our existence. This is the beginning of all communication—communication from God, who loves us before we love him. We come from the Father.

In discovering the Father we become *thinkers*, we awaken thought in ourselves, which is the following of the light of truth, walking with the Son, the Logos incarnate, leading to the face-to-face knowledge of the Father that only the Son possesses, and those with whom he shares it.

The sharing is done through the Spirit, the *Ruah* or breath of the Father that carries the Word. The breath is the atmosphere, the conversation, the kiss by which the two are united in giving and receiving. It is the way we follow ('The wind blows where it wills, . . . so it is with everyone who is born of the Spirit,' John 3: 8). 'Communication' is closely related to 'communion.' The Spirit is the Rhetoric of God.

These are the theological foundations of this approach, expressed as succinctly as possible. But of course we are not aiming at an education that will exclude all but theologians and believers. The theology helps us understand our humanity, including our needs and desires; the purpose of education is to enable that humanity to grow and flourish. The first chapter will make that clearer by focusing our attention on the heart of the school, and the relationship of pupil and teacher.

A Key to the Book: Eight Threes

Mythos	Logos	Ethos
Grammar	Dialectic	Rhetoric
Remembering	Thinking	Speaking
Music/dance	Visual arts	Drama
One	True	Good
True	Good	Beautiful
Given	Received	Shared
Father	Son	Spirit

I

Child, Person, Teacher

At the Heart of a Catholic School

A GREAT DEAL has been written about education without much consideration being given to the nature of the child. Of course, there has been plenty written about the *developmental psychology* of the child, but that is not quite what I mean. Social-scientific approaches have their place, but they are no substitute for one based on the lived experience—which we all share—of once having been a child, and of knowing children. Philosophy and theology have as much light to throw on this experience of being a child as psychology, sociology, or neuroscience.

What I am reaching for in this chapter is a balance between two philosophies of education that have been at war in our society for over a hundred years: what we might call the 'romantic' and the 'classical' tendencies; the tendency to become entirely child-centered *versus* the tendency to become entirely teacher-centered. Each side reacts to the excesses of the other, and yet the conflict can be avoided if we base ourselves on a more adequate and complete appreciation of the human nature both of the child and of the teacher. These must be understood as bound together in a relationship that transcends them, in service of a reality to which they both belong.

Revival of the Trivium

The modern revival of the Trivium or language arts was influenced by a famous essay called 'The Lost Tools of Learning,' by Dorothy L. Sayers (best known for her fictional detective, Lord Peter Wimsey). Sayers associated each of the three 'ways' or arts—which she terms Grammar, Logic, and Rhetoric—with a particular stage of child development.[1]

The *Grammar* stage corresponds, Sayers thought, to that time in childhood when we love to learn things by heart, to chant nursery rhymes, and of course to learn words. It is well known that very young children possess an ability to learn multiple languages that is generally lost as they grow older. Teaching in this stage revolves around rhythmic games, including word and number games. The foundations of arithmetic and geometry are laid through play concerned with simple numbers and shapes, and through learning the 'times tables' which link the two. This is the *Sesame Street* stage of education, based on memory, which Sayers called the 'Poll Parrot' stage.

The *Logic* stage is concerned less with collecting facts than with relating them together in a framework that begins to make sense. The child can move on from lists of numbers and words to algebra and logic, from simple sentences to arguments and paragraphs, from lists of events and dates to the more complex historical narratives that connect them. Dorothy L. Sayers called it the 'Pert' stage, because the child is beginning to form opinions and may assume those opinions are always right.

Finally, the *Rhetoric* stage completes the whole process by teaching how to make an argument convincing to others, and how to communicate our own experience to the wider world. It is what Sayers called the 'Poetic' stage. We might also call it 'romantic.'

All this is intuitively quite appealing. It reminds us we must accommodate education to the needs and capacities of the child,

---

1 Dorothy L. Sayers, 'The Lost Tools of Learning,' 107–35. In modern schools that have tried to revive the classical curriculum, these three phases of learning have been found useful in constructing a curriculum. Wisdom and virtue are cultivated by nourishing the soul on truth, goodness, and beauty embodied in great books and works of art. The student is encouraged to perceive, attend, and remember the beauty in a great work, understanding it sufficiently to re-present it in an original form, or apply the idea in a new situation. Socratic dialogue-style techniques are used to develop the ability to criticize, to develop an independent view, by bringing hidden assumptions to light and examining possible implications.

provided these are realistically understood. But I dare to say that realism has not been a hallmark of recent educational theory and practice. In most countries educators are polarized between two approaches. On the one hand, the old-style, classically-minded educators regard teaching as mainly a matter of conveying information (reading, writing, and arithmetic, plus in a Catholic context salvation history, moral commandments, and the deposit of faith). Much of this is to be learned by heart, backed up by a system of discipline involving examinations and penalties. The revival of this approach is periodically stimulated by panic at falling literacy levels and suchlike. On the other hand, 'romantic' educators believe that too much rote learning and compulsion will turn children against education altogether—and in Catholic circles away from the Church.

Romantic educators insist on an experiential style of teaching based on active learning projects, the teacher's job being mainly to provide encouragement and suitable resources, such as stories, games, ideas, and (very occasionally) information.[2] Thus in English schools, even very good ones, recent years saw a tendency not to teach 'correct' spelling or grammar, on the grounds that the child should first acquire the love of self-expression. In American schools, prioritizing the need to bolster a child's self-esteem has led to such absurdities as pupils being given certificates of recognition for 'future achievements' that may never happen, and a refusal to award low grades or admit failure. (This is equivalent, in the moral and sacramental context, to dropping the teachings on sin, on the grounds that God can forgive anything and wants all to be saved.)

The romantic approach often ends up encouraging narcissism, overconfidence, and vacuous sentimentality. It gives an inadequate formation in basic skills, and undermines the determination to do well. Catholic teachers who merely encourage a child to pursue his or her own unique 'faith journey' without also

---

2 For a defense of the traditional teacher-centered method of education, as opposed to the 'romantic-progressive' approach, see Michael C. Zwaagstra, Rodney A. Clifton, and John C. Long, *What's Wrong with Our Schools and How We Can Fix Them.*

teaching the elements and showing the coherence of faith, are making a fundamental mistake. Certainly there is a journey to be made in faith and to faith, but there is in Catholicism a certain content that cannot be found simply by searching, discussing, and arguing. It is called revelation. To take Catholicism seriously is to accept the authority of the Church to teach us what we could not know otherwise. On the other hand, it has to be said that the more classical educational style has a downside too. It may discourage intelligent inquiry, leading to the privatization of religion and a growing sense of irrelevance. A 'cultural' Catholicism that is kept going by little more than force of habit or nostalgia evaporates when the pressures imposed by school or family are released. So how do we find a new balance, a new approach that does justice to the positive in both of these methods of education?

Centering Education on the Child

It may help to glance at how this tension or conflict came about during the last few centuries, before we discuss how it may be resolved.

The modern period saw a transformation of educational theory and practice in favor of child-centered education. In the wake of the temperamentally Romantic *Jean-Jacques Rousseau* (d. 1778) and as an extension or manifestation of the Romantic movement in general, modernity became associated with a growing respect for the particular nature and development of the child. Insight into the value of the child can be traced back to Christ, though it remained mainly implicit during most of the succeeding centuries, and it seems that before the eighteenth century childhood was often considered merely a stage of weakness and immaturity to be got through as quickly as possible. Rousseau himself—not a great educator, but a considerable influence through his novel *Emile*—believed in the natural goodness and value of the child, wanted education to be adapted to each new developmental stage, and placed great emphasis on the importance of the child's activity or active involvement in the process. We can trace his influence through several of the best-known educationalists of the succeeding centuries (though a discussion of two of the most important, *Charlotte Mason* and *John Holt*, will be postponed until the chapter on education in the family, Chapter 6).

A century after Rousseau, *Friedrich Froebel* (d. 1852) is best known for his invention of the *kindergarten*, which was conceived as the center of an interactive educational process based around the activity of the young child. (The idea of a 'garden' fitted with the romantic notion that the child was like a plant that needed nurturing, rather than a receptacle that needed filling.)[3] Believing that children have an innate desire to learn, he concluded that the 'game' is the typical form of life in childhood, and play is the key to education, capable of laying solid foundations for the adult personality. ('Play is the highest expression of human development in childhood, for it alone is the free expression of what is in a child's soul.') Children in the kindergarten typically learn through song, dance, gardening, and the use of geometrical and patterned blocks and toys—known as the Froebel 'Gifts.' These were supposed to represent the basic building blocks of the universe and the symmetries of the child's own soul.

The Froebel Educational Institute lists the main elements of this approach as follows. Its influence on much modern educational practice is obvious.

1. *Principles include* • recognition of the uniqueness of each child's capacity and potential • an holistic view of each child's development • recognition of the importance of play as a central integrating element in a child's development and learning • an ecological view of humankind in the natural world • recognition of the integrity of childhood in its own right • recognition of the child as part of a family and a community.

2. *Pedagogy involves* • knowledgeable and appropriately qualified early childhood professionals • skilled and informed observation of children, to support effective development,

---

3 Of course, although the organic metaphor is apt enough, 'the child-garden is an intolerable idea as failing to recognize the essential property of a child, his personality, a property all but absent in a plant' (Charlotte Mason, *Towards a Philosophy of Education*, 24).

learning, and teaching • awareness that education relates to all capabilities of each child: imaginative, creative, symbolic, linguistic, mathematical, musical, aesthetic, scientific, physical, social, moral, cultural, and spiritual • parents/caregivers and educators working in harmony and partnership • firsthand experience, play, talk, and reflection • activities and experiences that have sense, purpose, and meaning to the child, and involve joy, wonder, concentration, unity, and satisfaction • holistic approach to learning which recognizes children as active, feeling, and thinking human beings, seeing patterns and making connections • encouragement rather than punishment • individual and collaborative activity and play • an approach to learning which develops children's autonomy and self-confidence.

Whereas Rousseau was a freethinker and Froebel a Lutheran,[4] *Don Bosco* (d. 1888) was a Catholic priest and became a saint. His approach was akin to theirs in some ways, and yet crucially rather different in others. Loving children as much as any romantic, he was more concerned than Rousseau with their fragility and moral danger—more aware, let us say, of the legacy and implications of original sin than most of the romantics. His educational philosophy was intended to produce 'good Christians and honest citizens'; that is, good citizens on earth in order to become good citizens in heaven. For Bosco, nature and grace are not opposed, but interpenetrate for the sake of a final goal that is the supernatural fulfilment of the natural. Education must serve the supernatural dignity and destiny of the child, allowing it to blossom in the social dimension.

Bosco rejected the repressive approach to education in favour of a preventive approach based on friendship, appealing directly to the heart and to the innate desire for God ('reason, religion, and

4 Both Rousseau and Froebel of course had predecessors, notably the seventeenth-century Protestant (Moravian) encyclopedist John Amos Comenius, himself influenced by Jacob Boehme on the one hand and Francis Bacon on the other, whose idea of universal education 'according to nature' was expressed in the textbooks he wrote and schools he organized in Sweden, with lasting effect especially in Scandinavia.

loving-kindness' was one formulation, 'cheerfulness, study, and piety' another). His pedagogy made use of music, theatre, comedy, walks, and excursions. Though this approach is still child-centered, it places a great responsibility on the person of the educator, since the young person is not expected to flourish naturally in this world without a relationship that offers personal attention and genuine love. But in this context, if such a relationship can be established, grace is able to flow and the development of reasonableness, imagination, empathy, and conscience is much more secure. It involves a kind of partnership between child and teacher.

Another significant figure is *Rudolf Steiner* (d. 1925), the founder of Anthroposophy and the inspiration for a thousand Waldorf Schools around the world. The schools began in 1919 when Steiner was invited to create one for the children of workers at the Waldorf-Astoria cigarette factory, based on the ideas in his 1909 book, *The Education of the Child.* Steiner believed in the need to educate with the spiritual as well as emotional, cultural, and physical needs of children in mind, and taught that they progress through a series of developmental stages corresponding to the evolution of human consciousness itself. Abstract and conceptual thinking develops late, around the age of fourteen, and so the early years are more focused on art, imagination, and feeling. Subjects tend to be presented in a pictorial way, usually involving music, rhythm, routine, and repetition (exposure to television and computers is minimized). The system relies on a strong relationship with a class teacher who normally stays with the same children from ages seven to fourteen. Prior to that, the children attend a kindergarten where child-led play alternates with teacher-led activities in a carefully structured environment. The Upper School curriculum fosters independent thinking and is taught by specialist teachers.

Waldorf Schools are run collegially rather than by a head teacher, and assessment is by the teachers' observation of the children in their care rather than by formal examination. The children are helped to compile their own lesson books by hand in the Lower School, which prepares them for independent note-taking in the later phase. In general, this holistic approach seems to work—children are happy and sociable, and academic standards are often judged to be higher than in conventional main-stream schools. Particularly valuable is the emphasis on seeing 'parts' in the context of 'wholes,' and connecting the topics taught with everyday life and experience through art and craft—that is, by engaging the child's senses and imagination in the process of learning.

The Italian doctor, *Maria Montessori* (d. 1952), like Bosco a Catholic, developed her ideas around the same time as Steiner—by 1907 she thought she had discovered the true 'normal' nature of the child by working with the disabled, and her work subsequently was to create an environment in which children (especially young children, up to the age of six) could help to direct their own learning. The normalization of the child took place through a state of deep concentration, evoked by some task of the child's own choosing. The younger child has an immense capacity to absorb experiences and concepts that become foundations of the later personality, and a particular sensitivity to music, although, in common with most educational theories, abstract reasoning was held to develop later. The curriculum in a typical Montessori school or play-group is not pre-set, but consists in a series of challenges introduced by the teacher when the child seems ready for them.

The biggest influence of all, though he lacked the spiritual depth of the others, is probably the American empiricist and pragmatist *John Dewey*, who died in the same year as Montessori (1952). His books on education from 1897 to 1938 argued that the purpose of education was two-fold: the realization of the child's full potential, and the facilitation of social change—education being the midwife of democracy. In 1915 he wrote these rather telling words that later became a charter for the progressive movement in the United States: "children should be allowed as much freedom as possible.... No individual child is [to be] forced to a task that does not appeal.... A discipline based on moral ground [is] a mere excuse for forcing [pupils] to do something simply because some grown-up person wants it done."[5] Realizing too late some of the dangers in the overly child-reliant

5 John Dewey, *Schools of Tomorrow*, 211.

approach, he tried to develop his notion of experiential education to balance the interests and experience of the pupil against the importance of subject content and the role of the teacher as a partner in the process of learning. The focus was supposed to be less on the child and its cognitive development than on a theory of experience (the interaction of past experience with present to facilitate learning and the growth of an ability to think for one-self). But it seems that Dewey's approach remained too theoretical, and was easily manipulated by those who wanted to use education to change society for ideological purposes.

What can we learn from this? Great educators differ in their conclusions about the nature of the child and the developmental stages that need to be taken into account, and even about the nature of the learning process, but each tries to devise an environment in which the child's natural, impulsive quest for knowledge—or for beauty, goodness, and truth—can be pursued with the teacher's help. The basis for a good education is, on the one hand, the self-motivation of the child to pursue what engages and interests him, and on the other, the creativity, responsiveness, and love of the teacher, who sets the terms for learning and encourages the child to flourish. If the romantic tends to underestimate the effects of the Fall, he is at least correct that children retain a desire to learn that needs to be encouraged. But a framework conducive to learning—as the classical approach sometimes emphasizes to excess—must include the habits of discipline and attention without which such desires are easily dissipated. It is important, too, without being too rigid about it, to appreciate that different stages of development have different needs. An emphasis on educational play may be less appropriate at a stage when more solid content is required.

To Be a Child

We all know there is a child still within us. That child may be ignorant, selfish, immature, confused. It may be desperately in need of love it has never received. But it is innocent and pure. I think it was in that sense that Georges Bernanos wrote:

What does my life matter? I just want it to be faithful, to the end, to the child I used to be. Yes, what honor I have, and my bit of courage, I inherit from the little creature, so mysterious to me now, scuttling through the September rain across streaming meadows, his heart heavy at the thought of going back to school.[6]

Christianity has given a particular importance to childhood. It certainly transformed, over time, the way children were perceived in classical civilizations.[7] From the statement of Christ, 'Whoever does not receive the kingdom of God like a child shall not enter it' (Mark 10:15), it followed that there was something valuable and to be imitated in the state of childhood. Throughout human history, children had been told to grow up and become like adults, not the other way around. For Christ there is no contradiction between being mature and being childlike.

In fact we find in the Gospels very little about our Lord's childhood, except the incident in the Temple when he was lost by his parents at the age of twelve, and then his response to them demonstrates considerable maturity—while his words and actions in adulthood show a childlike spirit that never leaves him.[8] Childhood is an undeveloped stage, but in some ways it also represents a more perfect state, when we can see more completely what it is simply to be human. Until Mary Immaculate (in the words of Bernanos, 'younger than sin'),[9] no one had lived that human existence perfectly, but in her and in her newborn Child we see what it is to receive one's being straight from the hand of God and to show forth what it is to be loved and to love.

This is not to romanticize or idealize childhood, but to understand it in the light of a new fact: the Incarnation of the second person of the divine Trinity. God has a Son. We are made in God's image. The child, as Christ taught implicitly when he

---

6 Cited in John Saward, *The Way of the Lamb* (99), which contains a developed theology of childhood.

7 This history is traced by C. John Sommerville in *The Rise and Fall of Childhood*.

8 See Hans Urs von Balthasar, *Unless You Become Like This Child*.

9 Cited in Saward, *The Way of the Lamb*, 117.

productive. Not only can we not rely on the policing of corridors for the preservation of purity and the development of conscience, these are far from the best way to begin. The soul needs love, as the positive force around which all its powers will congregate. It needs a degree of tenderness, if it is to flourish without fear. It needs attention, in the sense that others—the teacher especially—must listen to it and be receptive to what it has to offer, if it is to discover for itself what that is.

Attention

The greatest teachers I have known have been able to give that quality of attention. It is as though they possessed the awareness of which C.S. Lewis famously writes in *The Weight of Glory*—the awareness that there are no 'ordinary' people, no average children.

> It is a serious thing to live in a society of possible gods and goddesses, to remember that the dullest and most uninteresting person you talk to may one day be a creature which, if you saw it now, you would be strongly tempted to worship, or else a horror and a corruption such as you now meet, if at all, only in a nightmare. All day long we are, in some degree, helping each other to one or other of these destinations. It is in the light of these overwhelming possibilities, it is with the awe and the circumspection proper to them, that we should conduct all our dealings with one another . . . , all friendships, all loves, all play, all politics.

Or as Thomas J. Norris writes, 'In the face of every boy and girl before me there is mirrored the mystery of his or her origin, the potential for his or her itinerary through life and society, and the promise of a success, not only earthly, but above all transcendent.'[12] It is a serious thing to be a teacher, just as it is a serious thing to be a parent. (In both cases the burden of responsibility would be too great for us if it rested on our shoulders alone. Luckily the destiny of the child does not depend on us.)

12 Thomas J. Norris, *Getting Real About Education*, 25.

If attention to the child is the key to the teacher's success, it is the child's own quality of attention that is the key to the learning process, or so Simone Weil asserts in her 'Reflections on the Right Use of School Studies.'[13] She almost goes as far as to say that the subject studied and its contents are irrelevant; the important thing, the real goal of study, is the 'development of attention.' Why? Because *prayer consists of attention*, and all worldly study is really a stretching of the soul towards prayer. 'Never in any case whatever is a genuine effort of the attention wasted. It always has its effect on the spiritual plane and in consequence on the lower one of the intelligence, for all spiritual light lightens the mind.' An attempt to grasp one truth—even if it fails, and even in a seemingly unrelated subject—will assist us in grasping another.

> Every effort adds a little gold to a treasure no power on earth can take away. The useless efforts made by the Curé d'Ars, for long and painful years, in his attempt to learn Latin bore fruit in the marvelous discernment that enabled him to see the very soul of his penitents behind their words and even their silences.[14]

Attention is desire; it is the desire for light, for truth, for understanding, for possession. It follows, according to Weil, that the intelligence 'grows and bears fruit in joy,' and that the promise or anticipation of joy is what arouses the effort of attention: it is what makes students of us.

Making known to the child or student the special way of 'waiting on truth' in every problem, whether in language or mathematics or any other subject, is what Weil identifies as the first duty of the teacher. For this makes it an exercise in 'waiting on God,' which God will one day reward with tenderness. 'Every school exercise, thought of in this way, is like a sacrament.' School studies have a higher purpose than the acquisition of information or worldly skills. These acquisitions will follow, but

---

13 Simone Weil, 'Reflections on the Right Use of School Studies with a View to the Love of God,' 44–52.

14 Ibid., 46.

they are subordinate to the orienting of the soul to God, implicit in the act of attention.

To my mind, in these remarks Simone Weil has put her finger on the essence of education, and practically on the essence of Christianity itself. The love of God is of the same substance, she points out, as the love of neighbor. Both are 'attentive,' based on a way of looking that requires the soul to empty itself of all its contents 'in order to receive into itself the being it is looking at, just as he is, in all his truth.' This is the truth that sets us free, that turns us from servants into friends. The teacher must model this attentiveness for the student, by loving him in the same way.

The attentive concentration on that which is sought and desired unites teacher and pupil through the presence of the 'third,' which is the living truth (the 'content,' if you like) not yet possessed and yet somehow invisibly present, implicit in the relationship itself. The relationship is what makes the truth flow. We learn because we love. The teacher's job is to bring about that relationship, that state of attention, or to be aware of it and nurture it when it arises, by loving the child.

A Catholic Philosophy of Education

While part of the problem with modern education has been an extreme tendency to center everything on the child to the exclusion of actual instruction (the problem of content-free, pupil-centered learning), it is true that education is about the *human person*, and finding ways to enable that person to flourish through a certain quality of attention. The unity of knowledge that we seek in our vision of education has its center in the person, understood as a kind of relational existence with others. This is also the key to achieving the right balance between the child and the teacher, since both, viewed as persons, are part of something larger than themselves. So before we look in detail at the meaning of the Trivium, let us focus on this general principle, and its bearing on the nature and ethos of the school (education in the home will be discussed later).

'Personalism' is a name we give to a philosophy that gives priority to the person as distinct from the individual. Here the 'indi-

vidual' means the particular human being thought of as possessing an identity quite separate from others, and as entering
into relationships with them—if at all—by choice. The 'person,'
on the other hand, means the human being determined in his
identity (from within, as it were) by *relationships* both chosen and
unchosen. The relationships into which we are born—with our
family, our village, our tribe, or our nation, and above all with
God—help to make up our identity as a person, but hardly count
for the 'individual' at all. The individualist thinks of himself as a
free-floating atom or particle, whereas the personalist is content
to be bound up in a molecule or part of a body with other atoms
(which is not to say that such bonds may not ever be dissolved or
transferred).

The personalist tendency is found in a wide range of Catholic
authors in the past century or so, from Jacques Maritain and
Emmanuel Mounier to Dietrich von Hildebrand and John Paul
II. Thanks to the latter it can be said finally to have gone main-
stream. In doing so it became closely allied with the *ressourcement*
movement which sought to return to the sources of tradition
(Henri de Lubac, Louis Bouyer, Hans Urs von Balthasar). This
broad movement of Catholic thought gives us a new understanding firstly of the human being, secondly of the relationship
between nature and grace, and thirdly of beauty in its relationship to truth and goodness.

First, it consists in the insight that we are creatures of freedom,
by which we shape our own destiny. Our nature is determined by
relationship to others, and is fulfilled by the gift of self in love.
This is connected with the second set of insights concerning
grace, for it turns out that human freedom and the power to love
is itself a gift, by which we are enabled to share in the freedom of
God. Furthermore, our freedom has no ultimate fulfilment
which is purely 'natural,' but is satisfied and perfected only by the
giving of the self to its supernatural object: God. The life that is
ours by nature, as persons, is therefore not opposed to the life of
grace or supernatural gift. (What is opposed to grace is sin, a mis-
use of freedom which destroys the harmony of nature and grace.)

These first two developments were consolidated by the
authoritative documents of the Second Vatican Council in the

1960s. They were taken a stage further theologically by Hans Urs von Balthasar, who explored the underlying form of the grace that fulfills the world. This is where 'beauty' comes into the picture. In the divine object of love he saw the mutual coinherence of truth, goodness, and beauty.

Of course, none of this is really new. It is all implicit in the writings of the Fathers and Doctors of the Church, right down to that 'Doctor' of our own age, Blessed John Henry Newman. Though implicit, it remained for a long time undeveloped within the Church, hidden under a crust of dry Scholastic theology. The renewal of theology in our day turns it back into what it was for the Fathers and Saints, a science of love, at one and the same time precise, systematic, and practical. Love has been rescued from the marshes of sentiment and reinstated as the bedrock of God's revelation to humanity, a revelation about nature, ourselves, and God.

In Catholic personalism, the inner structure of love is revealed as Trinitarian. In any complete act of love the self of the lover is simultaneously given, received, and shared. To be united with another through love is not to lose one's distinctive identity, but to be confirmed in it. From her knowledge of the structure of love, derived from a meditation on the revealed Trinity, the Church is able to unfold a comprehensive ethical and social teaching, according to which human society is understood as a *communio*: that is, a communion of persons called to fulfilment in mutual service or solidarity. And by virtue of the fact that physical bodies belong to our essence as persons, this solidarity extends to the very limits of the natural world.

Developments such as these in theology give some hope of a renewal to come in education, if ways can be found to apply them in practice. They should help to dissipate any sense that religion is irrelevant to everyday life, or that it is opposed to science. They should provide a basis on which to defend the objectivity of standards and a framework of absolute values within education. The same set of developments should help to ensure respect for the freedom, inviolable conscience, and personal experience of each student, by valuing persons above mere ideas and information. Furthermore, they deepen our understanding of the role of authority in the teaching process.

Given the widespread modern antipathy to the very idea of authority, a word more is needed to expand that last remark. Essentially, Catholic personalism gives the notion of *obedience* a spiritual value,[15] but far from subjecting us to the whims of every tyrant who comes along, this sets limits to any merely human authority by placing it in ordered relationship to the divine authority who rules all things with justice and mercy.

A person must become detached with respect to the self, in order to become capable of unreserved attachment to God as the soul's true center. The student submits to a teacher, not out of respect for the teacher's personal qualities, which may sometimes be hard to discern (I once had a teacher who chased his pupils around the school to beat them with a slipper), but out of respect for the role or office—in other words, for the authority the teacher is commissioned to represent. The teacher must therefore be the one who submits first. He must submit to God, and to the objective truth he hopes to teach. It is only in the name of that prior obedience, and the limitations it implies, that the teacher has a right to demand obedience of the student. It follows from this also that genuine authority must grow in proportion to humility (as the example of the saints demonstrates beyond all doubt).

A personalist philosophy of education therefore starts from the premise that the human person should be educated for relationship, attention, empathy, and imagination. The school (which receives its authority over children ultimately from their parents) does not exist simply to feed the industrial machine with workers, or the market with consumers. It is oriented towards the family and family life. The process of education certainly involves the communication of useful information and skills, but only in the context of an initiation into a community of relationships extending through time, the family first of all, then broadening to the lived experience of a cultural tradition. The more human we become, the more our own lives and experience connect with different aspects of the culture into which we are progressively initiated by the school.

---

15 The root of the word *obedience* means to 'listen' or 'pay attention.'

According to the Parable of the Sower (Mark 4:1–20), faith is like a seed: it needs fertile ground in which to grow, but once it is grown, it transforms both the soil in which it was planted and the landscape around it. The ground, however, is important. Dry, shallow soil is not good enough to set down roots. In the same way, we may make our schools and homes inhospitable to the seed of faith by depriving our children of the experiences, the culture, and the language in which faith may be received and supported and nurtured.

To make the content of the curriculum relevant to the everyday life of the pupil, it is essential not to shrink the content to match the pupil's present experience, but to expand the life of the pupil to match the proposed curriculum. The key is the fact that to grow as a person we must learn self-transcendence. For Christianity, a world centered on the ego must give way to a world centered on the other(s). And in this process, the *ethos* of the school is always at least as important as its curriculum and teaching methods. Growth in prayer and in love is at the heart of education, for prayer involves interior opening to the supreme Other. It is the relationship to God made possible by this opening that strengthens us in our attempts to know and love the whole creation, and our neighbor as ourselves.

II

Remembering

Grammar — Mythos — Imagining the Real

'Language is the house of being. In its home man dwells.'[1]

WITH THIS CHAPTER, I begin to examine in detail the first three of the traditional liberal arts, namely Grammar. I want to connect this with the art of Remembering.

In Greek mythology, the goddess 'Memory' (Mnemosyne) is the offspring of the primordial Mother and Father; that is, Earth (Gaia) and Sky (Uranus). She is responsible for the naming of things, and is the mother by Zeus of the nine Muses, who inspire literature and all the arts, from poetry to astronomy. Memory, then, is the mother both of language and of civilization. This is what gives us our link between Remembering and language.

It was the Greeks who invented Grammar. Kenneth L. Schmitz writes that it was they who, 'by an effort of mind and imagination, withdrew partially from the immediacy of their spoken language in order to lay it out before themselves and to dissect or analyze its functional elements: eventually into nouns, verbs, adjectives, adverbs, prepositions, moods, conjugations, and declensions.'[2] Out of Grammar developed both Dialectic and Rhetoric. 'Grammar is the cradle of all philosophy, and in a manner of speaking, the first nurse of the whole study of letters,' says

---

1 Martin Heidegger, 'Letter on Humanism' (1949), in D.F. Krell (ed.) *Martin Heidegger: Basic Writings*, 193.

2 Kenneth L. Schmitz, *The Recovery of Wonder*, 16–17.

John of Salisbury in 1159.[3] It was Grammar that enabled the Greeks to enter more deeply into the reality of the cosmos, not just by becoming conscious of how language functions, but by becoming conscious of themselves as inventors, users, and refiners of language.

The actual word Grammar comes from the word *grammatikos*, meaning 'letters.' One who masters the grammar of a language has developed the skill of interpretation, of reading symbols made up of individual letters and sounds, which build to whole words and texts. The exegesis of Scripture, of works of art, and even of nature herself might be included as an extension of this idea. As Pope Benedict XVI writes in his third encyclical:

> *Nature expresses a design of love and truth.* It is prior to us, and it has been given to us by God as the setting for our life. Nature . . . is more than raw material to be manipulated at our pleasure; it is a wondrous work of the Creator containing a 'grammar' which sets forth ends and criteria for its wise use, not its reckless exploitation. (*Caritas in Veritate*, 48)

I decided to discuss Grammar under the heading of Remembering to emphasize the link between language and memory. It is not simply that the mastery of words requires an act of remembering sufficient to associate each word with a particular thing (naming), or to recall the way individual words build into statements and questions. Certainly that is true. But there is a more profound sense in which to fill a word with meaning is an act of *remembering the being of the thing itself.* I take sides here with the

---

3 John of Salisbury, *The Metalogicon*, 37. John goes on to explain that 'Man's mind first applied names to things. Then, reflecting on its own processes, it designated the names of things by further names, to facilitate the teaching of language and the communication of thoughts from one mind to another. A word which is declinable, but lacks tenses, is called a "noun" if it signifies a substance or in a substantial way, whereas one which formally, so to speak, refers to what is present in a substance, or something along this line, is called an "adjective". . . .' (41), and so on with verbs, both active and passive, to represent temporal action, and then words of secondary application. The point being that Grammar begins with naming and proceeds from there by way of self-consciousness and reflection upon language itself.

Platonic-Augustinian tradition, where the act of defining an essence is guided by an intuition of being—of how this particular thing belongs to the whole from which we all come.

In Plato's dialogue *Meno*, Socrates famously has some fun with a slave boy who has never studied geometry, drawing out from him by a series of questions the right answer to a complex geometrical problem. The questions do not put the truth into the boy's mind but help him to discover it there. (It is supposed to be an example of the method Socrates habitually employs.) Socrates concludes that the soul already knows all things—moral as well as mathematical—before birth, and simply has to *remember* them. As a proof the demonstration hardly seems effective to modern ears, but what Socrates is really talking about is the function of a teacher, which is to raise a student from the state of confusion and ignorance to a state of knowing. It is the job of the teacher to lead the student to that interior place where he can see the truth for himself—just as a great sculptor might claim that his art is simply to remove enough stone to reveal the beautiful form within. Truth once known is 'seen' in the substance of the soul. Socrates therefore claims that 'searching and learning' are a process of *anamnesis* or recollection (81d), and the dialogue looks forward to the *Phaedo* (72e–77a) where the theory of the Forms is presented: in learning we come to recollect, to remember, the Forms such as Beauty, Even and Odd, Justice, and so on, that are permanently present in that Original Being or 'pre-existence' which is our own origin.

Naming: The First Human Task

Through language we demonstrate and activate our humanity, and channel the faculties of memory, imagination, and thought. For George Steiner, language is at the root of freedom, and the more languages we know, the freer we are to speak and conceive the world in different ways (as he says, 'The polyglot is a freer man'):

Language creates: by virtue of nomination, as in Adam's naming of all forms and presences; by virtue of adjectival qualification, without which there can be no conceptualization of good and evil; it creates by means of predication, of chosen remembrance (all 'history' is lodged in the grammar of the past tense). Above all else, language is the generator and messenger of and out of tomorrow. . . . Above the minimal vegetative place, our lives depend on our capacity to speak hope, to entrust to if-clauses and futures our active dreams of change, of progress, of deliverance.[4]

But freedom is not simply a matter of imagination and of future and conditional tenses; it is much more truly a matter of relationship, of 'I' and 'Thou.' This, too, is reflected in the dynamics of language (especially if Wittgenstein is right about the impossibility of a purely private language). The archetypal moment of language is that of *naming*, which overcomes the gap between the self who names and the thing that is named. It is this that enables us to 'inhabit' the world in a completely new way.

'[W]e have to be clear about what a name actually is,' writes Pope Benedict XVI. 'We could put it very simply by saying that the name creates the possibility of address or invocation. It establishes relationship. When Adam names the animals, what this means is not that he indicates their essential natures, but that he fits them into his human world, puts them within reach of his call.'[5] And behind all naming, all invocation and evocation, as Steiner suggests, lies the possibility of transcendence—the 'real presence' of an Other beyond all others, an Other who is *calling us* to discover or create meaning in the world. The act of speaking, of saying, is a 'wager on transcendence.'

The account in Genesis also describes the man's discovery of what Pope John Paul II called 'original solitude' (Adam's awareness of his otherness from the rest of creation), and 'original unity' (his awareness that he shares that uniqueness with woman) as the basis for an imaging of the Trinity through marriage.[6]

Thus in Genesis 2:18 God reflects: 'It is not good that the man

4 George Steiner, *Real Presences*, 56.
5 Joseph Ratzinger Pope Benedict XVI, *Jesus of Nazareth*, 143. The idea that names might be descriptions of the true natures of things is one that Plato explores playfully in *Cratylus*.
6 See Carl Anderson and José Granados, *Called to Love*.

should be alone; I will make him a helper fit for him.' This is the first time God has said 'not good' about something in his creation. Even so he is not saying that man or man's state is not good, but that it *would* be not good if he were to remain alone. But before revealing man's 'helper,' he must display every other possibility and parade them before him. 'So out of the ground the LORD God formed every beast of the field and every bird of the air, and brought them to the man to see what he would call them; and whatever the man called every living creature, that was its name' (Gen. 2:19).

We must remember that the act of naming was not understood in the ancient Hebrew and Christian tradition as a matter of merely 'attaching a label.' It represents something much more like appointing a place in the world, or giving a mission—as when Jesus named Simon the *Petrus* (rock) on which he would build his Church. In Greek the word *nomos* contains the meanings of both 'name' and 'law.' It may be that what Adam is doing by naming the other creatures is simply *ruling*, as he was intended to do: ruling not for his own selfish aggrandizement, but in accordance with the reality of things and with the wisdom of God. He was put into the garden 'to till and keep it' (Gen. 2:15), and to 'have dominion over the fish of the sea and over the birds of the air and over every living thing that moves upon the earth' (Gen. 1:28). The naming of the animals is an essential part of his vocation.[7]

As the friend of C.S. Lewis (and Christian Platonist) Charles Williams puts it in his novel, *The Place of the Lion*:

> By the names that were the Ideas he called them, and the Ideas who are the Principles of everlasting creation heard him, the Principles of everlasting creation who are the Cherubim and Seraphim of the Eternal. In their animal manifes-

---

7 The original state of justice or harmony between man and the rest of nature in paradise is sometimes glimpsed even in the fallen world, when in the presence of a person of special sanctity such as St Francis or St Cuthbert, the animals show something of the friendship and obedience that they did toward Adam.

tations, duly obedient to the single animal who was lord of the animals, they came.

The living universals were intended to circle around the Man who is the 'balance and pattern of all the Ideas.'

Man the Mediator

Naming is our first task, our mission. It is to connect the Ideas in God and the things in the world. We are to be the mediator, the recognizer. The Ideas are somehow in us, or we could not recognize them. Made in God's image we are also an image of the whole world. The other creatures reflect the same reality but more partially, in a fragmented way. It is man who puts the pieces together, who sees how they belong and where they should go. In the boy who goes out in the fields to spot the different kinds of birds, or collects the names and numbers of trains passing a certain platform, or collects stamps, lovingly pasting them into an album according to country of origin, we see the echo of this universal human mission still continuing.

The birth of language, expressed in mythopoetic form in Genesis, takes place within a specific context: the yearning (*eros*) for a 'helper' to make all things good—that is, for a companion in life who will reveal man's own nature and destiny to him. 'The man gave names to all cattle, and to the birds of the air, and to every beast of the field; *but for the man there was not found a helper fit for him*' (Gen. 2:20).

In other words, Adam could not find among the other creatures a lover, a face able to respond to him and look into his eyes as an *equal*. Only an equal is worthy of the gift of self. It is this that God now provides, from out of man's own substance. According to the Genesis account, the move from language as naming to language as interpersonal communication is marked by a cry of joy addressed to God:[8] 'This at last is bone of my bones and flesh of my flesh; she shall be called Woman [*ishshah*],

8 It should be noted that the naming takes place not in isolation but in the presence of God and in response to God's invitation or challenge.

because she was taken out of Man [*ish*]' (Gen. 2:23). In naming Woman he comes to self-consciousness by recognizing a shared nature—for she is his helper in all the tasks pertaining to humanity. In naming her, and therefore himself (*ish*), he also becomes aware of the necessity of governing himself. Now begins the drama of human freedom, which is a drama of the Fall and Redemption, of exile and return.

Historically, and in evolutionary terms, the birth and development of language is still mysterious to us. But, whether or not Noam Chomsky was right to suppose a universal grammar, the Old Testament speaks of a time when 'the whole earth had one language and few words' (Gen. 11:1). The story of Babel and the division of tongues refers to the process by which we forgot this primordial speech—a language that possessed 'few words' because each word was capable of bearing much more meaning than those of our own age (a power we glimpse only in the greatest poetry today). Some ancient writers suggest that the languages or races into which mankind was symbolically divided after Babel number 70 or 72, equivalent also to the number of the Names of God. Implied here is the idea that the words of the primordial language (which is also the language of the angels) consisted simply of the divine Names. Since all qualities found in creation pre-exist in God, those Names must contain everything worth saying about anything.[9]

However, we cannot ever actually *name* God, because that would imply that we had some kind of power over him. It would imply that the finite could comprehend the infinite. In fact, the most archetypal act of naming is not Adam's naming of the animals, but God's naming of himself. In the encounter with Moses

---

9 Cf. Valentina Izmirlieva, *All the Names of the Lord*. The 'primordial language' was not ever spoken by men in a literal sense, but refers to the one Word in which all things are contained, the Logos of God, communicated to the Christian community at Pentecost as 'tongues of fire.' Sound and light are symbolic of the same reality; that is, the spiritual vibration by which being and meaning are communicated. The names which are the 'forms' of existence manifested in the act of creation are pre-contained in the unity of the divine essence. On traditional philology see Ananda Coomaraswamy, '*Nirukta* = *Hermeneia*.'

at the burning bush, God names himself 'I am.' He tells the reluctant prophet, 'Say this to the sons of Israel, "I AM has sent me to you"' (Ex. 3:15). God's name is himself. It is so sacred that the Jews only allowed the High Priest to pronounce it once a year in the Holy of Holies. It is the act of Being, the primordial act of language, the principial Word.

Thus it is not we who name him, but God who names himself, or rather who gives us sacramental tokens to use as names—tokens of his presence: such as 'I am,' 'Jesus,' and 'Abba,' for example. The many other names by which human beings try to identify an object for worship, such as 'the Just' or 'the Merciful,' and even 'the Creator,' describe only aspects of him, paths of approach, angles of sight; like colors in a rainbow compared to the white light of the sun.

We cannot name God, and there is one other I cannot name. It is myself. Of course, each of us is given a name in the world, and we use it to locate ourselves among family and friends, but this is only a starting point. Adam names himself 'Man' only in relation to 'Woman.' Our own self is always more mysterious than we realize, and never less mysterious than when it seems to have been reduced to something known and thoroughly classified. In the end it is God who will name us, rescuing us from the prison of being known by others, giving to those who are saved from destruction 'a white stone, with a new name written on the stone which no one knows except him who receives it' (Rev. 2:17), and placing on their foreheads the name of God himself (Rev. 23:4); for seeing his face, they shall become like him.

All of this suggests that the earliest stage of education is not simply the learning of words, of names, of vocabulary, but the learning of *how to name*. This is the art that the poet re-learns, and so it can best be taught by teaching the power of poetry, and of *poesis* in general—both by learning and by doing (though we will come back to poetry under the heading of Rhetoric later). The power of naming is related to the power of seeing; of seeing into the realities, the essences of things, and invoking those essences by an act of will—and therefore of *interpretation*. The inversion and distortion of this power can be seen in the ability of names—nicknames, for example—to hurt and wound. By naming someone in cruelty we draw attention to some trivial or undesirable aspect of their person and identify them by this characteristic. It is a technique we all remember from our schooldays, and for some it may blight the experience of life for years to come. The Grammar we must learn is the opposite of this. It is a way of using language to praise, to celebrate, to magnify.

The experience of Eden is the experience of the dawn of language and the making of human consciousness, the remembrance of being, and of seeing into the essences of things through words newly minted. The world of creatures is blazing with glory against a background of absolute darkness. And if the world no longer blazes for us, perhaps it is our fault. 'We are in Eden still; only our eyes have changed.'[10]

Recollecting and the Spirit of Tradition

In the Beginning [the *arche*] *was the Word* [the *Logos*], *and the Word was with God, and the Word was God* (John 1:1). In that Beginning, in that Word, is the secret of our own origin. Over time we travel far from God, although the Beginning never departs from us for a single moment, and indeed is travelling with us, an invisible breath bearing us along. We are sent into the world from God, and the fulfillment of our nature is to return to him bearing gifts that we have made our own to give him. The return to the Beginning is accomplished through *anamnesis*: 'Do this in *anamnesis* of me,' says Jesus at the Last Supper. The word means 'memory' or 'remembrance,' but also 'recollection,' even 'reconstitution'— not just a going back into the past, but a gathering together into the present.

The formal study of the history of words and their meanings is called etymology (from *etymon* or *etymos*, 'true sense' and *logos*, 'word' or 'speech'). The student of language is called a 'philologist,' a lover of the *logos*. Etymology is important, if we want to find the springs and furnaces where words are forged, and understand why they are so important to our humanity. We must travel this path as lovers ('amateurs') of the Word and of words,

10 G.K. Chesterton, *The Defendant*, 3.

44

because all things reveal themselves more truly to the eyes of love.

In his Word, God recalls us to our home. Remembering Jesus, becoming members of his body, we are remembered by him, written in his Book of Life, located where we can never be forgotten. The theme of remembering and forgetting is interwoven with that of the Covenant, our familial relationship with God in the Hebrew and Christian scriptures. To be absent from the Covenant is to be forgotten by God; it is to be an exile, homeless in the cosmos. These facts are written into our nature and into all human experience.

Whenever we return home we are remembering. There is no home without memory to make it so; there is only a place like any other. Even an orphan raised on the streets remembers a face, a shelter, which represents where he comes from. My 'home' may have been brutal, the memories of it may make me cringe with fear, but it cannot ever be fully left behind, unless I can replace it with something other and better. All through life we are seeking a place where we can be at home, where we can truly belong. If we cannot remember that experience of belonging, then we are forced to remember something that defines it by contrast. Either way, it is memory that defines our journey.

It is not just as individuals that we need a home. The collective memory of the society to which we belong has the name 'tradition.' We cannot be truly 'at home' without one. The word derives from trans- 'over' and dare 'to give.' In every society or civilization, a process takes place that can be called a 'handing over' of the stories, the knowledge, the accumulated wisdom of one generation to the next. It is the process that makes each new generation into a source of wisdom for the one that follows— and it takes place generally within the family. What is handed over is a 'gift.' It is not simply a bundle of property whose title deed is being transferred to the next generation. Rather, it carries within it something of the giver. Its transmission is an act of love. Thus the gift of tradition involves and transforms the interiority of both the giver and the recipient.

Tradition in the sense I am describing is of the highest value because it is not something we simply manufacture, nor something cooked up by our parents, but something our parents themselves have received with gratitude and respect. Its origin ('the Beginning') is what makes it sacred. Some kind of revelation of truth, or what is believed to be a revelation, forms the seed of every great tradition, mediating between our own individual origin and that of the greater world. Tradition is venerated because of this. The moment we suspect that our tradition is based on a lie is the moment it loses its authority over us. Thus tradition is based on the act of faith. I adhere not simply because it has been handed down to me, but because I believe it is true, even if I cannot directly verify its truth for myself.

The 'spirit of tradition' is an essential element of education. It is the spirit in which the transmission of culture takes place. (It can be introduced to the child through folk songs, local history, and family history, for example.) This allows the initiation of succeeding generations into the truth that binds them together. The receptivity proper to love makes possible the transmission of tradition from one generation to the next. And when that spirit is present, tradition is never felt like a dead weight on the present. Only a tradition that has lost this spirit can become a deadening force.[11]

In much of the modern world, tradition is perceived in exactly that way—as deadening. The implications for education are immense. In traditional societies, the past is a living part of the present, continually rehearsed, celebrated, and interpreted

---

11 Josef Pieper, in *Tradition: Concept and Claim*, stresses the fact that tradition is not expected to change or progress over time. By its nature it is something that must be handed down faithfully and intact. I would qualify this by adding that 'development' (in the sense explored by John Henry Newman) does in fact, and should, occur in tradition, but only organically, so that the essence of the tradition remains intact. And, as Hans Urs von Balthasar writes, 'To honor the tradition does not excuse one from the obligation of beginning everything from the beginning each time' (*Razing the Bastions*, 34). Furthermore, since we adhere to tradition believing it to be true, we must also be prepared to purge it of anything we discover to be false. In that case, the spirit of tradition would only insist that we do so with respect, and without jettisoning important truths at the same time (the discernment of which is a matter of delicate judgment).

through ritual and story. Tradition joins the generations together in a community of *anamnesis* that transcends time. The contemporary dissolution of the family is also the dissolution of tradition, because it can only be passed on within the community whose identity it helps to define.

Anti-Tradition and Anamnesis

Our technology also tends to eliminate tradition, and with it the possibility of a truly human *living in time*. If human memory and knowledge is evacuated into cyberspace, the past too becomes something we treat as external to ourselves, something other than us, something we sit back and observe. The self then contracts into a point, and ceases to dwell in the world by being extended through time. It is no longer fully embodied. It becomes a detached observer of the grid of knowledge, an insatiable consumer set loose in an infinite supermarket of information.

Technological consumerism at its worst thus threatens to become not just the enemy but the perfect inversion of tradition. Whereas tradition requires the initiation of persons into a living world that is received as gift and calls for gratitude, anti-tradition converts the world into a pattern of information that can be transferred instantaneously from one mind or computer to another, in exchange for money. The purpose of tradition is to serve the personal growth and development of man. But the purpose of the mechanical order that currently dominates education is for man to serve the growth and further evolution of the machine.[12]

---

12 Romano Guardini gives a fuller analysis of this in *The End of the Modern World*. He thinks the medievals were concerned not so much with the rational or empirical investigation of nature (this was a later obsession), but rather—on the basis of revelation and ancient authority—with constructing a *symbolic cosmos*. The cosmos provided the necessary imaginative mediation between the world as experienced around us through the senses and the world of true ideas and essences, the world to which the contemplative intellect gives access. But under the impact of technology, our knowledge of nature becomes increasingly indirect. The elimination of the symbolic cosmos seems to have been necessary to focus on the development of the scientific method, but it has several unfortunate effects—including the reduction of religion to ideology.

The Last Supper, and the *anamnesis* with which Christ charges his disciples—a perpetual 'memorial' handed down in a living fashion through the apostolic succession of bishops and priests from then until now—gathers together the elements of a cultural tradition, along with the personal experiences of the disciples who have found their home with Jesus, and elevates all this to the level of a sacrament, a ritual that enacts the Trinity and unites us afresh with the Beginning of all things. This is the moment when tradition becomes Covenant. Christian or not, we can see in the scriptural narration of this event a mystery opposed to the technological order, the possibility of overcoming the essence of consumerism through consumption of the Eucharist, the gift of a supreme love that creates and nourishes a new communal identity. In the *anamnesis* of the Eucharist we are present to God, present to ourselves, present to each other.

Our first educational challenge is to counter the corrosive effect of technology on the traditions that nourish our humanity by *anamnesis*. If the spirit of tradition is to be preserved and revived, liturgy is going to be the key, for this is the school of memory, the place where we recollect ourselves, where we learn how to relate to each other in God. This is where we learn to accept the past and existence itself as a gift calling for a response of gratitude. Prayer and worship are therefore not extraneous but should be a central element in the life of the school or family. As we pray, so shall we be.

Defending the Art of Memory

Towards the end of Plato's dialogue *Phaedrus*, Socrates discusses the merits of speech as contrasted with writing. Writing, he suggests, has a tendency to 'implant forgetfulness' in the souls of men (275). Relying on external marks on paper to call things to mind, they will lose their capacity to recall things from within themselves. They will seem to know much, but mostly will know nothing, being filled not with wisdom but with the conceit of wisdom, thinking themselves to be better than they are.

Furthermore, he goes on to say, whereas living speech is addressed and directed to a particular person in all his particular circumstances, written speech can only sit there passively and be picked up and used at the whim of anyone, appropriately or not. Dialectic respects the transcendent nature of truth, which must be discovered together or not at all. The written text pretends to master and contain the truth, which in reality exceeds anything that one person can grasp. Speech, like music, requires time to unfold naturally, whereas the written text is laid out all at once on the page, like an inadequate image of eternity.

Plato's critique of writing calls into question the whole myth of progress that shapes our view of human history. His concerns seem to have been borne out by the decline of memory after the development of printing, and even more since the invention of the internet. Of course, there is a case to be made on the opposite side. There are certainly advantages to writing things down, and often great clarity can be achieved in no other way. The writing down of the wisdom of the ancients—not least of Plato himself—and its transmission by the Arab scholars and Christian monks of the Middle Ages enabled civilization to triumph over barbarism. Socrates may not have written anything down except in the souls of his hearers, but Plato himself is composing a dialogue in written form. Nevertheless his irony conceals a profound point. The spoken word, with the direct communication of soul to soul it signifies, ultimately has priority over the written, and the written must always in a certain way defer to it.

Also, it is true that reliance on the technology of writing eventually empties the human soul of much of its content. I remember being told at school (and it was a great comfort to me at the time) that it was not necessary to remember any actual facts as long as I knew *how to look things up in a library.* Today, in a world with instant access to Google, we rely on the electronic web to supply everything we need, from historical facts to word definitions and spellings as well as extended quotations. All of us who use a computer are aware of the shock of inner poverty that we suddenly feel when deprived (by a virus or other disaster) of our mental crutches even just for a day or a week. Plato is right: memory has been stripped from us, and all we possess is an external reminder of what we have lost, enabling us to pretend to a wisdom and an inner life we no longer possess in ourselves.[13]

The lessons for education are clear: reliance on computers is dangerous, and there is a case for banning them altogether from certain stages of the educational process, encouraging students to memorize what they need, and to analyze and take notes based on their own remembering and hearing rather than resorting to the laptop or sound recording (and similarly to throw away for a while the electronic calculator and instead work things out the difficult way).[14]

We are faced with the task of recovering what we have lost, or at least of countering some of the pernicious effects of an over-reliance on modern technology. But how is this to be achieved? By bringing back rote memorization in schools, and by testing students on their recall of information? Partly, no doubt, but it is worth noting that there is also implicit in Plato a critique of 'rote' memory. True human memory is not mechanical repetition; it is an organic assimilation and appropriation. What is remembered is something other than the self, but something experienced and known through the self. This means that we must probe a little more deeply into the meaning of memory, before we try to work out how to recover it.

The Christian Platonists, and especially St Augustine, gave their notion of memory the deepest foundation possible—within the Trinity itself. Within our human nature, made in God's image, Remembering, Augustine says, resembles the Person of the Father. The Father comprises the entire divine nature, begetting the Son as perfect self-knowledge, and united with him in the perfect love of that which is perfectly lovable (the Holy Spirit being, in a sense, the mutual love of Father and Son). Without the Father, God's act of self-knowledge would have nothing to reflect upon. Memory is a bit like that. And just as the Persons of the Trinity are distinct yet inseparable from each other, so our *remembering* is inseparable from our *knowing* and *loving*, which resemble

---

13 The point is developed in persuasive detail by Nicholas Carr in *The Shallows: What the Internet is Doing to Our Brains*, especially 144–8; 171–98.

14 See Endnote 3.

the Son and the Spirit. (This implies that if we fail to remember the whole of ourselves, we know ourselves imperfectly, and love in a fragmentary way, distorting the image of God.)

Augustine's influential analogy is worked out primarily in the tenth book of his *De Trinitate*. In the fourteenth he goes on to say that the truer analogy—the perfection of the image of God in us—is not when we remember, understand, and love ourselves, but when we remember, understand, and love God. This again connects the notion of memory and its cultivation with our discussion of liturgy.

> This trinity of the mind is not really the image of God because the mind remembers and understands and loves itself, but because it is also able to remember and understand and love him by whom it was made. And when it does this it becomes wise. If it does not do it, then even though it remembers and understands and loves itself, it is foolish. Let it then remember its God to whose image it was made, and understand and love him. To put it in a word, let it worship the uncreated God, by whom it was created with a capacity for him and able to share in him. In this way it will be wise not with its own light but by sharing in that supreme light, and it will reign in happiness where it reigns eternal.[15]

Thus by speaking of Memory or Remembering we are really speaking of the foundations of attention, of the integration of the personality, and of the road to contemplation. We are also speaking of 'conscience.'[16] Remembering is the gathering-together of the self in the light of consciousness, which in us

---

15 Augustine, *The Trinity,* 383.

16 See Endnote 2. There I mention that 'Guardini speaks of the practice of "recollection" as the awakening and living of one's unique soul as the only way to give life its meaning and purpose.' In 'Conscience and Truth,' Joseph Ratzinger identifies the 'first level' of the human conscience with Platonic *anamnesis*, which he describes as the capacity to recall 'what my nature points to and seeks' (534–5)—the attraction to the Good, which is also my Origin. The second level is that of judgment and decision. I may be culpable not only for my decisions, but for the 'neglect of my being which made me deaf to the internal promptings of truth' (538).

tends to be a piecemeal process, but in God is complete and 'instantaneous.' For us, therefore, the training of memory is essential if we are to discover and enlarge our human identity in the image of God. It is an essential foundation for any education worthy of the name.

However, the ability to remember is not a faculty that is already perfected in us, but a seed that has to be nurtured and directed to its true end. Can this ability be improved by training? The early Jesuits might have something to teach us on this point. It was they who developed the 'art of memory' to its highest pitch, in the sixteenth century—a skill with which Matteo Ricci greatly impressed the Chinese Emperor and his court. The technique seems to have been based on the close relation between memory and imagination. In the mind's eye, a 'memory palace' could be constructed, and particular items to be memorized were then stored in the various rooms and compartments of this palace. All that one needed to do to remember a particular thing was to go to the appropriate room, and open the appropriate drawer.[17] (No doubt if you are averse to palaces, a garden with bushes, trees, and flowers would do just as well.)

The Hall of Fire

As we move from individual words to the construction of sentences we have begun the making of narrative, of stories; and stories, like names, reveal the meaning and relationship of things to ourselves. The *anamnesis* of culture and tradition is largely dependent on our ability to remember and build upon the stories that come down to us. These stories are the *vehicles of meaning*.

J.R.R. Tolkien tells us that it was in fairy-tales that he 'first divined the potency of the words, and the wonder of the things, such as stone, and wood, and iron; tree and grass; house and fire;

---

17 A history of memory techniques can be found in Francis Yates, *The Art of Memory*. Kevin Vost's book, *Memorize the Faith!*, contains practical instructions for the teaching of these techniques today. Also recommended as an introduction to the subject is Vincent Cronin's novel about Ricci, *Wise Man from the West*.

bread and wine.'[18] To be enchanted by story is to be granted a deeper insight into reality: 'By the forging of Gram cold iron was revealed; by the making of Pegasus horses were ennobled; in the Trees of the Sun and Moon root and stock, flower and fruit are manifested in glory.' Thus Frodo, on first seeing the Elvish land of Lothlórien, can only describe it in terms of a new language:

> A light was upon it for which his language had no name. All that he saw was shapely, but the shapes seemed at once clear cut, as if they had been first conceived and drawn at the uncovering of his eyes, and ancient as if they had endured for ever. He saw no color but those he knew, gold and white and blue and green, but they were fresh and poignant, as if he had at that moment first perceived them and made for them names new and wonderful.[19]

But we do not have to look as far as fairy-tales. The simplest sentence consisting of subject, object, and verb tells a story. Take, for example, 'I love you,' or 'The dog sits.' These combinations of words tell stories that are simple, but no less profound than the great sagas told around the world. A child gazes into the world with an intensity and purity that wonders at the smallest event. A ball rolls across the carpet. The sun comes from behind a cloud. The waves beat on the shore. In such events are revealed archetypes, for those with eyes to see. God is revealing himself. Being is unveiled. As we grow older, we need more elaborate stories to achieve the same effect.

The Hall of Fire in Rivendell (foreshadowed in Tolkien's earlier posthumously published writings as the 'Cottage of Lost Play') represents the place where tradition is passed on through story, where meaning is revealed, where language expresses itself in the making and interpretation of worlds. The ambience of fire, of a friendly hearth where all strangers are made welcome and find consolation, speaks of a place where humanity can take root and

---

18 J.R.R. Tolkien, 'On Fairy-Stories,' in *Poems and Stories*, 167. For more on Tolkien see my *The Power of the Ring* and (with Tom Honegger) *Tolkien's Lord of the Rings: Sources of Inspiration*.

19 *The Lord of the Rings*, 369.

flourish, a true home—the 'Last Homely House.' Here prose is subordinate to poetry, and poetry to song. (Such places had and have a central place in many cultures. Tolkien was drawing on the ancient Scandinavian and Germanic tradition of the mead hall, or *meduseld* in Old English; a hall built for feasting, hospitality, storytelling, and song.)

From his schooldays, Tolkien possessed a keen sense of his mission as a poet. He shared with other English Romantics the sense that something vital had been lost from our civilization in the new industrial and scientific age. That something was a poetic consciousness, a mode of knowing through feeling and intuition that connected us with nature and with the natural law, with the reading of God's intentions expressed in nature and the divine wisdom manifest in creation. He believed we had become increasingly alienated from nature (the natural world around us and increasingly our own human nature as well) by our determination to know it solely by conquest, through experiment and measurement. He would have supported the educational idea that children should be brought up on a rich diet of folklore and story, with plenty of experience of natural, growing things in the garden and countryside.

Tolkien fulfilled his poetic mission to some extent by means of his fantasy writing, as I intimated earlier, with the help and support of small groups of friends that he formed or joined at various points in his life, the last and most famous of which was C. S. Lewis's group, the Inklings. One of this group's members, Owen Barfield, was not an orthodox Christian, as Tolkien was and Lewis became, though he did regard Jesus Christ as the central figure in world history.[20] His book *Poetic Diction* was read and admired by Tolkien, as it was by Lewis, and his view of Romanticism more or less describes the 'project' of the Inklings. According to Barfield in *Romanticism Comes of Age*, the Romantic Movement had so far missed its vocation, but in Coleridge,

20 Owen Barfield's best-known book is *Saving the Appearances: A Study in Idolatry* (1965). It surely belongs on a shelf with other seminal works such as C.S. Lewis's *The Abolition of Man*, Richard Weaver's *Ideas Have Consequences*, and Josef Pieper's *Leisure the Basis of Culture*.

Goethe, and (especially, he thought) Rudolf Steiner it leads us towards a new stage of human consciousness. Romanticism has two aspects, he thinks: literary and metaphysical. In the former, it is associated with a mood of strangeness and distance evoked by the phrase 'over the hills and far away.' In the metaphysical aspect, it is associated with the power of creativity and a growing sense of freedom, together with a concern about the nature of goodness, and a tendency to trust imagination as an organ of perception. Hovering between the two aspects is *beauty* as an object of human devotion.

The tragedy of the Romantics, according to Barfield, is that beauty became disconnected from truth. Objective truth was claimed by the empirical sciences, whose great successes in the nineteenth century left most of the Romantics feeling powerless and resentful. They lost themselves in a world of feeling. Only in Goethe, in his theory of color and of morphology, does one see an attempt to bridge the gap. Johann Wolfgang von Goethe (d. 1832), writing as a scientist as well as a poet, proposed a new empirical method based not on the analytic reduction of wholes to parts but on the imaginative observation of the wholes revealed in the parts. Here is 'poetry approaching science with outstretched arms,'[21] and yet they do not quite embrace, not yet. It is a point to which C.S. Lewis directs some attention at the very end of his book *The Abolition of Man*, when he speaks of the possibility of a 'regenerate science' (no doubt reflecting conversations with Barfield which go back to a time before his own conversion to Christianity).[22]

Tolkien's unfinished story 'The Notion Club Papers' was written two-thirds of the way through *The Lord of the Rings*, around 1945.[23] In it, one of the characters, Ramer, claims to have been hearing and re-learning in his dreams what he calls his 'native language'—not an earthly language in the ordinary sense, but the translation into earthly sounds of some more basic and word-

---

21 Ibid., 34. On Goethe's philosophy of science, see Henri Bortoft, *The Wholeness of Nature*.

22 An account of them can be found in Lionel Adey, *C. S. Lewis' 'Great War' with Owen Barfield*.

less form of communication. He thinks this is what people are unconsciously trying to reconstruct when they feel compelled to make up 'beautiful languages of their own in private'[24] (as Tolkien, notably, did). Like Barfield, Tolkien believed the evolution of human consciousness is reflected in language.

In essence, Tolkien was trying to recover the vision of Eden, the childhood of the race, when beauty was still connected with truth. Through story—the *right kind of story*, including traditional legends and fairy-tales—that ability to see all things with a pure heart and in the light of heaven could be evoked. He wanted to prove that poetic knowledge, George MacDonald's 'wise imagination,' could be awoken even in a world apparently closed to its very possibility.[25]

Music of Creation

I have tried in this chapter to loosen Grammar from the narrow confines of an association with sentence construction, to show that the birth of language is bound up with memory and poetry and the telling of stories about the world and about ourselves. None of this is to deny the importance of careful instruction in syntax, vocabulary, or the other aspects of classical and medieval Grammar, taught using the great written works of our tradition.

23 See J.R.R. Tolkien, 'The Notion Club Papers,' in *Sauron Defeated*, 145–327. It purported to be a document from the future, being based on a bundle of papers tied with red string and found among the waste paper in Oxford's Examination Schools in 2012. Written in the 1940s, the Papers recorded the imagined conversations of an academic club meeting during the 1980s.

24 Ibid., 201.

25 No wonder C.S. Lewis, on first reviewing *The Lord of the Rings*, described it as 'lightning from a clear sky' (C.S. Lewis, *Of This and Other Worlds*, 112). Malcolm Guite's *Faith, Hope, and Poetry* is a study of this Romantic 'counter-tradition' in English letters, in the light of which Tolkien's achievement makes more sense. Guite demonstrates the 'essential power of imagination to bridge the gap between immanence and transcendence, to mediate between unembodied "apprehension" and embodied "comprehension"' (243). On the relevance of the mythopoetic consciousness of the English Romantics to the contemporary 'deconstruction of deconstruction' (the placing of Enlightenment rationalism in doubt by the situating of science in an anthropological context), see Keith Lemna, 'Mythopoetic Thinking and the Truth of Christianity,' 69–98.

Without close attention to the evolving structure of language, our reading of texts will fail to reach what the author was trying to say; and our ability to communicate our own thoughts will suffer just as much. Without the training to handle words with precision and accuracy we will fail to express our own thoughts or communicate them to others. But there is more to Grammar than this. Our experience of the world is full of meaning from the moment we begin to connect our experiences with each other by remembering and comparing and imagining. Words are the tokens of images, and it is as such that they mediate human interpretation and thought. We unveil the meaning of the world to ourselves by comparing one thing with another, by getting the 'measure' (*logos*) of it, by seeing one thing as 'like' or 'unlike' another, and so by learning to dwell in the mysterious space that is formed between them. The human soul, we might say, is this intermediate reality, this 'interworld' of meanings and connections.

For Barfield, the development of each child recapitulates the evolution of consciousness in the human race over millennia. As soon as the child has begun to distinguish the 'I' from the 'not I,' he discovers words as a medium of communication. He moves from concrete, wordless thinking to abstract, logical thinking.

> But between these two there is an intermediate stage, at which consciousness takes the form of pictures or images. In the history of mankind that intermediate stage contains the mystery of the Myth. It still contains to-day the mystery of Poetry, and with that the whole great mystery of Meaning. It is Imagination. Imagination is the marriage of spirit and sense.[26]

It is in the Imagination that language and the Muses are born from Memory in the house of tradition. The first lesson of our revised 'Trivium' is therefore the vital importance of crafts, drama and dance, poetry and storytelling, as a foundation for independent and critical thought. Through doing and making, through *poesis*, the house of the soul is built. The grammar of

26 *Romanticism Comes of Age*, 79.

language, however, rests on a deeper foundation still. It rests on *music*. Music is the wordless language on which poetry—the purest and most concentrated form of speech—is built. Poetry is made of images, similes, metaphors, analogies; but what holds these elements together and makes them live is fundamentally musical in nature.

In music we glimpse the grammar of creation itself, from the harmony of the planetary and subatomic spheres to the octaves of human experience and the cycles of growth in plants and animals. Modern writers as varied as Schopenhauer and Tolkien have seen the world as a kind of 'embodied music,' and of course the notion is ubiquitous among the ancients.[27] Music in turn is a play of mathematics, coherent patterns of number and shape in time and space, expressed in rhythm and timbre, tone and pitch. It is the closest most of us get to seeing and feeling the beauty of mathematics.

Our goal in education is a sympathetic or connatural knowledge of the true, the good, and the beautiful, rather than an abstract appreciation of values at a distance. For the ancient writers, this meant that education at every stage must be musical in this broad and deep sense. For Plato in the *Laws*, speaking through the Athenian, education as a whole is comprised of 'singing and dancing.' When the right kind of song penetrates the soul, the result is an education in virtue.[28]

---

27 So for example, according to Isidore of Seville in the seventh century (cited in E. M. W. Tillyard, *The Elizabethan World Picture*, 94), 'Nothing exists without music; for the universe itself is said to have been framed by a kind of harmony of sounds, and the heaven itself revolves under the tones of that harmony.'

28 *Laws* II, 672e, 673a. Earlier he has said that a musical education in virtue produces 'a keen desire to become a perfect citizen who knows how to rule and be ruled as justice demands.' Whereas a training 'directed to acquiring money or a robust physique, or even to some intellectual facility not guided by reason and justice, we should want to be called coarse and illiberal, and say that it had no claim whatever to be called education' (I, 643e, 644a). A later discussion in Book VII, 795e–804b, on the improvement of the soul or personality by music—as by the right kind of gymnastics, whether dancing or wrestling—and its integration in society with right worship, is also relevant here.

Rhythm, harmony, and melody—the subject of study at a more mature stage of a child's growth—must from the earliest age penetrate deeply into mind and soul through imitation and natural enjoyment. Only in this way, by ordering the soul in harmony and giving it a sense of the meaning of proportion and relationship, can it be induced later to become fully rational, and to derive pleasure from the theoretic contemplation of ideas. The road to reason leads through the ordering of the soul, which implies the necessity of an education in love, in discernment, and in virtue.[29]

If it is to take this deeper vision into account, the restoration of Grammar as one of the three elements of a restored Trivium must include not only the revival of memory and the discipline of learning by heart (*enlarging* the heart in the process), but the cultivation of imagination and a poetic or musical vision of the interconnectedness of all things. It is a harmony that cries out to be discovered and appreciated, repaying with joy the effort to reveal and understand it, and making us 'beautiful within.'[30]

We began by speaking about the act of 'naming,' which is the beginning of Grammar. From there we spoke about the act of naming as fundamental to our humanity. This led to a consideration of the art of memory and the meaning of tradition, the dangers of reliance on technology, and the importance of stories and storytelling (where I brought into the frame some English poets who have a lot to say on this topic). I argued that *Remembering* has to be understood as the beginning of our participation in a tradition of culture and learning, a community that transcends time and connects us with the origin of things. In this way 'Grammar' is transformed into the remembrance of Being. These are the deeper reasons we should study and teach the parts of speech, the syntactical structure of language, etymology, and other languages. The humanity of our children depends upon it.

29 Stratford Caldecott, *Beauty for Truth's Sake*, 38.
30 Plato, *Phaedrus*, 279c.

III

Dialectic

Thinking—Logos—Knowing the Real

*For language does not belong exclusively to the realm of myth; it bears
within itself, from its very beginning, another power, the power of logic.*[1]

LANGUAGE AND MYTH, bound up with our sense of personal
identity, destiny, and meaning, are rooted as we have just seen in
Remembering, but as soon as we come to self-conscious awareness we are of course involved also in Thinking, or the mental
processes by which we separate truth from falsehood. In this
chapter we move from the former to the latter—from Grammar
to the second of the liberal or language arts, traditionally known
as Dialectic or Logic; or let us say we move from the art of 'interpretation' or 'reading' (Grammar) to the art of analysis or *discerning the truth*.

At the same time, we move from the realm of *Mythos* to that of
Logos[2]—from the realm of the Father to that of the Son. The
threshold between Mythos and Logos is represented by the
words associated with the Oracle at Delphi (sometimes called
the 'womb' of ancient Greece), *Know Thyself*. Just as Apollo slew
the ancient Python, so light triumphs over darkness through dialectics.

The Logos is that intelligible order which may be seen in the
world and which comes from the Beginning or source of all
things. In that sense, it is referred to in religious teachings and
traditions under a variety of names, and it may well be implicit in

1 Ernst Cassirer, *Language and Myth*, 97.
2 See Endnote 4.

any 'religious' worldview insofar as religion is based on the veneration and celebration of meaning and order. Modern science seeks it in the form of a 'theory of everything'; a simple, elegant formula that would account for all known particles and energies and their interaction.

The Logos, which is necessarily a *universal* principle, is of course not the exclusive concern of Dialectic, nor is Dialectic merely another name for Philosophy, which along with Theology transcends all seven liberal arts as such. ('Philosophy' means the love of Wisdom, and we need all the arts to make the pillars of her house.) No, Dialectic is a more limited topic, though a central one in the history of Catholic education, and its relation to the others must be established as part of our search for its contemporary relevance.[3]

An Honorable Art

In his posthumously published doctoral thesis, *The Classical Trivium*, Marshall McLuhan undertakes a detailed history of the three arts of language, up to and including the Elizabethan writer Thomas Nashe, and what he has to say about their relationship to each other is of considerable interest. For McLuhan, 'In studying the history of dialectics and of rhetoric, as, indeed, of grammar, it is unavoidable that one adopt the point of view of one of these arts; and the history of the trivium is largely a history of the rivalry among them for ascendancy.'[4] The three arts are not 'left behind' as one moves up the educational ladder, but they remain foundational, and each of them can color one's whole approach to learning. Exponents of each take it in turn to subordinate the

---

3 John of Salisbury in *The Metalogicon* describes logic as 'the science of argumentative reasoning [rational discussion], which provides a solid basis for the whole activity of prudence' (74), but he goes on to spend several chapters criticizing those Academicians who devote their lives to Logic, mistaking the means for the end, and never acquire true knowledge. Dialectic 'is ineffective when it is divorced from other studies' and turned in upon itself (93). As I shall suggest, it must particularly not be separated from Grammar and Rhetoric.

4 Marshall McLuhan, *The Classical Trivium*, 41–2. See also Endnote 1.

others: rhetoricians subsume Dialectic under Rhetoric, dialecticians do the opposite.

Plato and Aristotle both sought to free dialectical argument from sophistry and therefore maintained its independence from Rhetoric, as did the Stoics, but Plato with his highly poetic, symbolic, and mythological style (despite his 'banishment' of the poets) is seen by McLuhan as the fountainhead of the grammatical tradition, rather than the dialectical or logical, for which the credit should go to Aristotle. For much of the Patristic and Medieval period Plato's influence was dominant, and the most respectable approach to truth was 'grammarian,' involving intuitive leaps and reasoning from analogy—as in the allegorical biblical exegesis of the Fathers. This tradition reached its peak in St Bonaventure, before being eclipsed by the more Aristotelian dialectical approach (after St Thomas, in whose work both methods are seen to advantage, but whose long-term influence was in favour of dialectics). McLuhan writes:

> As the method of patristic theology, grammar enjoyed uninterrupted ascendancy until the revival of dialectics by Gerbert, [Johannes] Roscellinus, and Abelard in the eleventh and twelfth centuries. With the decadence of dialectical or scholastic theology in the fourteenth and fifteenth centuries both grammarians and rhetoricians surge forward again, finally triumphing in the work and influence of Erasmus, the restorer of patristic theology and of the grammatical humanistic discipline on which it rests.[5]

After the Renaissance, the Rationalism of the Enlightenment submerged the grammatical tradition under a new synthesis of Dialectic and Rhetoric, taking its lead from Ockham, Peter Ramus, and Descartes. Grammar then 'fought back' through the Romantic movement—nourished in part by the subterranean streams of a Hermetic tradition which had kept the symbolic method of the grammarians alive.

What, then, is Dialectic, and why is it still important for the modern world, in which the conflict of Rationalism with Roman-

5 Ibid., 42.

ticism has blurred the boundaries and erased the distinctions between these three traditions? The conflict McLuhan describes between the three elements of the Trivium in Western thought prior to the Renaissance is largely due to the loss of a 'depth dimension' in which the three Ways might be seen as distinct yet convergent. At the level of methodology—on the flat plane, as it were—there is tension, if not conflict, between them right enough, and a continual jockeying for position. But to the extent all three Ways are concerned with rising *above the plane* to attain Truth, conflict gives way to complementarity.

In his Tractate on Dialectic, Plotinus, the founder of Neoplatonism, describes it as 'the precious part of Philosophy'—or, in Thomas Taylor's translation, 'an honorable part.' It is not the whole of philosophy, but it leads to Wisdom; it is an *instrument* of Philosophy, and Plotinus is at great pains to describe how it leads two types of human being, the 'musician' (or artist) and the 'lover,' step by step from the beauty that they can recognize—in a lovely picture or song, for example, or a desirable woman or man—towards the One Principle that is Absolute Beauty. Thus Dialectic in its true sense is not at all in conflict with Grammar (which leaps toward the Principle by intuition and analogy) or with Rhetoric (which provides the techniques by which the heart may be moved). It 'does not consist of bare theories and rules; it deals with verities [things]' and comes to rest in contemplation when its task is fulfilled.

> It is the Method, or Discipline, that brings with it the power of pronouncing with final truth upon the nature and relation of things—what each is, how it differs from others, what common quality all have, to what Kind each belongs and in what rank each stands in its Kind and whether its Being is Real-Being, and how many Beings there are, and how many non-Beings to be distinguished from beings. . . . Now it rests: caught up in the tranquility of that sphere, it is no longer busy about many things: it has arrived at unity and it contemplates: it leaves to another science all that coil of premises and conclusions called the art of reasoning, much as it leaves the art of writing: some of the matter of logic, no

doubt, it considers necessary—to clear the ground—but it makes itself the judge, here as in everything else; where it sees use, it uses; anything it finds superfluous, it leaves to whatever department of learning or practice may turn that matter to account.[6]

Encouraging Thought

The search for truth, in the sense of an ordered, coherent view of the world and its meaning, is fundamental to our humanity. Religion, science, and the arts all bear witness to it in their own ways. But the search is never easy, and our continued ability to *think coherently* cannot be taken for granted. Today, as mentioned, there are new threats that have to be taken into account.

> The digital age cuts back reading and, as a consequence, young people are losing the ability to think seriously. They get distracted more easily, breaking off to check an email. Speed-reading is exactly the wrong thing to do. You have to think about what you are reading. . . . You have to ponder.[7]

The opposite case could be made—that the new electronic media make writings of all kinds (including whole books) more accessible, and facilitate the ability to read and to assimilate the important elements of a text more quickly. However, the underlying point remains valid. To 'think' is not enough: you have to 'think about'; you have to ponder, rather than just flit from one image or phrase to another.[8] This is the second of the major concerns of our revised Trivium. We need to educate people to think coherently and independently—to take responsibility for their own thoughts.

6 *Enneads*, 1.3.5. The Taylor translation is available online from *www.theprometheustrust.co.uk*.

7 Noam Chomsky, cited at *http://findarticles.com/p/news-articles/sunday-telegraph-the-london-uk/mi_8064/is_20100704/quiet-anti-american/ai_n-54318674/*.

8 In the Bible, when Mary is described as 'pondering' these things in her heart (the mysteries of the Nativity), the word *symballousa* connotes a 'bringing together' to compare and examine.

Encouraging Thought

Thought in a child arises naturally. The job of the teacher is to encourage and defend it from being blighted and destroyed, to strengthen it and enable it to flourish. Education is more like gardening than manufacturing. As Margaret Atkins writes:

> Healing is done by our bodies; yet we need doctors. Growing is done by the plants; yet we need gardeners. Learning to think is done by young people. We need teachers, as we need doctors and gardeners, to provide and protect the conditions—in this case of good learning. This, I suggest, is done in three ways: by securing the appropriate environment; by guiding pupils towards the subjects and topics that are most worth learning; and by presenting ideas in an order that makes it easy for the learner to grasp for himself both this subject and its relation with others. It is obvious enough, I think, that these three tasks are essential to good teaching, but they can be so taken for granted that we rarely think about them directly.[9]

Here 'an appropriate environment' is one of 'calm, orderliness, and attentiveness' in which deep learning takes place, facilitated by a relationship of trust between teacher and pupil. The fear of punishment is not conducive to this kind of learning, but nor is the anxiety and stress induced by an obsession with grades and paperwork. As for the mentioned guidance of pupils towards subjects 'worth learning,' this implies that value-judgments need to be made—and not necessarily the ones built into a curriculum dictated by the State. The 'order' referred to here is the order of the world as comprehended through an adequate grasp of the whole. Thus the Logos is present implicitly throughout the syllabus. The teacher's job is to help the child make her or his own connection with this Logos.

A good teacher orders the explanation of a particular point in a way that builds a bridge between the truth of her subject and the individual mind of her pupil. She orders the topics within a subject, or at least appropriates and perhaps

9 Margaret Atkins, 'The Good Teacher,' *Second Spring*, issue 5 (2004), 35.

modifies the order provided by the curriculum. She is also responsible for ordering this subject in relation to others, so that her pupils can see how it fits into the wider intellectual tradition of her school.[10]

The child's head is more like an acorn than a jam jar, says Atkins. Teaching is not simply a matter of putting knowledge into it. This was discussed earlier. Learning is an active not a passive process. But it implies also that all learning is based in dialogue, beginning with the recognition of the Other and proceeding through the asking of the question, 'Why?'. The recognition of the Other and correspondingly of the Self—both contained within Being—corresponds to what I have called Mythos or Remembering (*anamnesis*), or asking the question 'What?'. The asking of 'Why?' is the dawn of Thinking.

Dialectics for Children

Children are natural Platonists (essentialists) *and* natural Aristotelians (empiricists). They jump to intuitive conclusions about the nature of the things and people they encounter. Like artists, or like grammarians, they connect things analogically. But they are also curious, inquisitive, exploratory, and they operate by trial and error. A baby will shove absolutely anything in its mouth until it works out what tastes good and what doesn't.

Children, in other words, have the balance just about right, and are naturally suited to the Trivium. Adults need to learn to do the same thing on a more sophisticated level. Someone who managed to do this was G. K. Chesterton. For me, Chesterton is a perfect example of someone who managed to attain as a grown-up the healthy wisdom and wondering appreciation of a child—a truly integrated man. He was not an academic philosopher but rather a journalist and a 'man of letters' (a man, in other words, of the Trivium). He enables us to see that Dialectics—that 'precious part' of Philosophy—does not belong merely in academe, but in everyday life. As the tools for our lifelong search for

10 Ibid., 37.

wisdom and truth, Dialectic belongs in the school and in the life of every child. In an essay called 'The Revival of Philosophy—Why?' he explains:

> Philosophy is merely thought that has been thought out. It is often a great bore. But man has no alternative, except between being influenced by thought that has been thought out and being influenced by thought that has not been thought out. The latter is what we commonly call culture and enlightenment today. But man is always influenced by thought of some kind, his own or somebody else's; that of somebody he trusts or that of somebody he never heard of, thought at first, second or third hand; thought from exploded legends or unverified rumors; but always something with the shadow of a system of values and a reason for preference. A man does test everything by something. The question here is whether he has ever tested the test.[11]

Chesterton's notion of 'philosophy'—which we here apply to that instrument of Philosophy called Dialectic—is 'thought that has been thought out'; that is, thought out by *someone*, but not necessarily the person doing the thinking (or speaking) at any given moment. The dialectician is the one who *thinks things out*, and Chesterton believes that each of us should do that for ourselves—or as many as possible should do that—since the alternative is to be guided by fragments of someone else's philosophy without ever realizing it. Chesterton is a great defender of individual freedom and responsibility, and clear thinking is one requisite of freedom. The same point is made by Blessed John Paul II:

> All men and women . . . are in some sense philosophers and have their own philosophical conceptions with which they direct their lives. In one way or other, they shape a comprehensive vision and an answer to the question of life's meaning; and in the light of this they interpret their own life's course and regulate their behavior. (FR, 30)

---

11 G.K. Chesterton, *The Common Man*, 176.

Of course, children—especially young children—are not able to 'think things out' the way adults do (although they often do a better job of it than we expect, and adults may do a worse one). But the rules of logical thought are relatively simple, even if we use long words to talk about them. The pattern of the syllogism, deduction, induction, and inference, a belief in the objective existence of a world other than myself, together with elementary notions of equivalence, fairness, reciprocity, and so on: these could be called principles of common sense, and they are evident in children from quite an early age. They can be illustrated quite easily from conversations in the playground or from storybooks. In 'Philosophy for the Schoolroom,' Chesterton explains how we can arrive at such principles.

> What modern people want to be made to understand is simply that all argument begins with an assumption; that is, with something that you do not doubt. You can, of course, if you like, doubt the assumption at the beginning of your argument, but in that case you are beginning a different argument with another assumption at the beginning of it. Every argument begins with an infallible dogma, and that infallible dogma can only be disputed by falling back on some other infallible dogma; you can never prove your first statement or it would not be your first. All this is the alphabet of thinking. And it has this special and positive point about it, that it can be taught in a school, like the other alphabet. Not to start an argument without stating your postulates could be taught in philosophy as it is taught in Euclid, in a common schoolroom with a blackboard. And I think it might be taught in some simple and rational degree even to the young, before they go out into the streets and are delivered over entirely to the logic and philosophy of the *Daily Mail*.

> Much of our chaos about religion and doubt arises from this—that our modern skeptics always begin by telling us what they do not believe. But even in a skeptic we want to know first what he does believe. Before arguing, we want to know what we need not argue about. And this confusion is

infinitely increased by the fact that all the skeptics of our time are skeptics at different degrees of the dissolution of skepticism.

Now you and I have, I hope, this advantage over all those clever new philosophers, that we happen not to be mad. All of us believe in St Paul's Cathedral; most of us believe in St Paul. But let us clearly realize this fact, that we do believe in a number of things which are part of our existence, but which cannot be demonstrated. Leave religion for the moment wholly out of the question. All sane men, I say, believe firmly and unalterably in a certain number of things which are unproved and unprovable. Let us state them roughly.

(1) Every sane man believes that the world around him and the people in it are real, and not his own delusion or dream. No man starts burning London in the belief that his servant will soon wake him for breakfast. But that I, at any given moment, am not in a dream, is unproved and unprovable. That anything exists except myself is unproved and unprovable.

(2) All sane men believe that this world not only exists, but matters. Every man believes there is a sort of obligation on us to interest ourselves in this vision or panorama of life. He would think a man wrong who said, 'I did not ask for this farce and it bores me. I am aware that an old lady is being murdered down-stairs, but I am going to sleep.' That there is any such duty to improve the things we did not make is a thing unproved and unprovable.

(3) All sane men believe that there is such a thing as a self, or ego, which is continuous. There is no inch of my brain matter the same as it was ten years ago. But if I have saved a man in battle ten years ago, I am proud; if I have run away, I am ashamed. That there is such a paramount 'I' is unproved and unprovable. But it is more than unproved and unprovable; it is definitely disputed by many metaphysicians.

(4) Lastly, most sane men believe, and all sane men in practise assume, that they have a power of choice and responsibility for action.

Surely it might be possible to establish some plain, dull statement such as the above, to make people see where they stand. And if the youth of the future must not (at present) be taught any religion, it might at least be taught, clearly and firmly, the three or four sanities and certainties of human free thought.[12]

The Search for Truth

Language, grammar, syntax, and vocabulary exist for a purpose, and that purpose is revealed only in the search for truth. As Chesterton saw, it is the search for truth that keeps us sane, because it always brings us back to reality. And why is reality so important? It is what we are made for. Reality is the food of the soul.

I said there are many kinds of truth, but of course there is in the end only one: *all that is the case.* The many poetic or scientific or psychological or aesthetic or probable truths that make up our intellectual landscape are simply aspects of, or means of approaching, the complete truth. It is fashionable to claim that ultimate or absolute truth is not attainable, or even meaningful, simply because people don't seem to be able to agree on what it is—in fact the scientific method does not even aspire to truth, only to hypotheses, always open (in principle, at least) to revision or replacement by something better. Part of the process of thinking is to learn how to set all these different types or approaches to truth in the right order, to see how they combine to give a more complete image of reality as a whole—to make it perfectly plain that we need poetry *as well as* science, imagination *as well as* reason, empathy *as well as* mathematics.

A 'madman,' in Chesterton's view, is someone who takes something that may well be true, or a method that may be valuable in its own place—logical inference, for example, or empiri-

---

12 *Daily News*, 22 June 1907.

cal investigation—and relies on this one thing alone to give him a picture of reality, as if we could infer the structure of the solar system using logic, or ascertain the strength of love by a laboratory experiment. 'The madman is not the man who has lost his reason. The madman is the man who has lost everything except his reason.'[13]

An education based on the traditions of the Trivium is one that never loses contact with the bigger picture, or with the multiplicity of ways in which human beings approach truth (affective, emotional, intellectual, intuitive). That is because it begins with Grammar, with Remembering, which means that it begins face-to-face with Reality. Thinking is anchored in this prior act, this receptivity to truth. Thought grows naturally with the use of language, where language is the awakening to consciousness of self-and-other in the community of Being.

In fact, much of the madness of the modern world—from which we hope to preserve our children by teaching them to think for themselves—can be traced back to a philosophical movement of the fourteenth century that rejected these principles, detaching Thought from Memory. Nominalists such as William of Ockham believed in 'naming' but thought of it as a purely human power, as the ability to stick labels on things rather than to recognize their true nature. They rejected the reality of 'universals' (such as man, lion, justice, and so on) on the grounds that only individual, particular things exist (a lion, a man, a just act). The universal idea is a fiction by which we try to group disparate things under a single heading. In the end, even the individual thing was destined to fall apart into a flux of elements—parts of the body, phases of existence, moments of time. The 'self' became as elusive as any other universal, any other label we affix

---

13 G. K. Chesterton, *Orthodoxy*. The second and third chapters of the book are all about this issue and deserve close study. The third concerns particularly the problem of Postmodernism: 'Just as one generation could prevent the very existence of the next generation, by all entering a monastery or jumping into the sea, so one set of thinkers can in some degree prevent further thinking by teaching the next generation that there is no validity in any human thought.'

to an ever-changing world, in order to impose some kind of order upon it for our own purposes.[14]

Some years ago, I was standing in what was left of the death camp of Auschwitz in Poland when the full implications of what the Nominalists had done finally hit me. No wonder the Jews could be treated as non-human, if 'human' is just a label we attach to a group of people we choose to relate to. And, further, no wonder so many people have no problem with abortion, if an embryo is just a cluster of cells to which we do not yet have to attach the label 'person.' For a philosopher such as Peter Singer, that label need not be attached until some time after birth, making infanticide once more thinkable. In this view, we become more human as we build relationships and acquire consciousness and skills. A man in a coma, an old drunk on the street, a convicted murderer, have no common humanity with a brilliant scientist or composer, a wealthy entrepreneur, or a young man with a wide circle of friends. There is no innate or infinite dignity attached to simply being human.

In a fallen world, and especially for us in the modern world, sanity has continually to be fought for—as Plato described Socrates fighting intellectually against the Sophists. It may be that these thinkers, who were teachers of *arête* (excellence or virtue, and therefore goodness), had once been interested in truth, and had been genuinely wise. But by the time of the Platonic dialogues they are portrayed as itinerant intellectuals interested mainly in money, peddlers of smooth phrases and techniques of

---

14 For details see Etienne Gilson, *The Unity of Philosophical Experience*, and Louis Dupré, *Passage to Modernity*. Richard Rorty offers a good example of where this tendency ends up: a 'philosophy' that explicitly renounces the search for truth (even its own) in the name of pure pragmatism, aiming only to serve the 'gratification of desires.' For an analysis of his position from the standpoint of the Platonic-Thomistic tradition, see Christopher Oleson, 'Rortian Irony and the Humility of Right Reason.' Oleson makes the important point that in this perennial tradition, it is clear that aspiration to truth and its attainment are dependent not merely on mental activity (no matter how 'brilliant') but on virtues of the soul such as purity and humility, which alone render us able to 'receive contemplatively the nature and end of things' (37).

manipulation, useful to the nobility for the sake of political advancement.

The dialogues in which the conflict between sophistry and philosophy is played out remain highly relevant to our own situation, when once again Truth has become separated from Goodness and Beauty. The Sophists of our day are the successors of the Nominalists. But how do we defeat them, when they are all around us?

Faith and Reason

Pope John Paul II never tired of making the point that education should be at the service of the human person, meaning the *whole* person, in whom the various branches of knowledge and study must come together in a universal vision, or at least an aspiration towards such a vision; a vision in which everything has its place, and everything has a vertical or interior dimension. In his encyclical on philosophy, *Fides et Ratio* (1988), he noted what had been lost, referring to the need for a recovery of 'metaphysical reasoning' and the 'philosophy of being.' We can use the encyclical as an introduction to the problem of philosophy in Catholic education, where the issue of the exact relation between faith and reason becomes paramount.

For John Paul II, each completes the other, in a sense contains the other, and enables the other to do its work. Faith opens reason to a transcendent horizon; it assures reason that the world as a whole does make sense; it encourages reason to aspire to a greater truth. Without the assurance of faith that the truth is somewhere 'out there,' reason would stop short on the journey, it would give up, it would lose itself at the foot of the mountain, as the Israelites lost themselves in the worship of the golden calf in the absence of Moses. At the same time, faith needs reason (and so theology needs philosophy) in order to penetrate ever more deeply into the mystery that has been revealed, to unfold its implications, and to explore the world in its light.

[B]iblical man discovered that he could understand himself only as 'being in relation'—with himself, with people, with the world and with God. This opening to the mystery, which came to him through Revelation, was for him, in the end, the source of true knowledge. It was this which allowed his reason to enter the realm of the infinite where an understanding for which until then he had not dared to hope became a possibility. (FR, 21)

In chapter 7 of *Fides et Ratio*, the Pope looks at the contemporary crisis in philosophy and issues a challenge to philosophers to resist tendencies to eclecticism, historicism, modernism, scientism, pragmatism, and nihilism. The details need not concern us too much here. Eclecticism simply means a lack of concern for coherent thought. Pragmatism replaces the criterion of truth with decisions based on utility. The beginning of this whole tendency is the loss of a sense of being and meaning, and its end is the nihilistic denial of the possibility of any knowledge at all. Thus the will to power, exercised above all through the development of machines, gradually takes the place of the will to truth and goodness. This is the situation of philosophy today, and the root of the crisis in our philosophy of education, as we have seen—the loss of the Logos that our Trivium must find a way to recover.

The Pope is careful not to deny, and on the contrary affirms, that modern philosophy has also achieved many 'precious and seminal insights' in its analysis 'of perception and experience, of the imaginary and the unconscious, of personhood and intersubjectivity, of freedom and values, of time and history' (FR, 48). He merely challenges philosophers not to abandon prematurely the search for truth, meaning, and coherence. Responding to that challenge today, I think we will need to venture into some fundamental philosophical questions. And we might start with one of the founders of philosophy in the post-Nominalist era, the Frenchman René Descartes, famous for the phrase *Cogito ergo sum* or 'I think therefore I am.'[15] If we are to develop a viable

15 What he means by 'thinking' is much broader than mere rational enquiry. He includes willing, judging, feeling, perceiving, as well as doubting, among our mental acts. In fact, by thinking he seems really to mean consciousness. Babies, and ourselves when we are unconscious, he says, may 'think' in this sense.

philosophy of education, we cannot avoid wrestling with his legacy, as many subsequent philosophers have done.

In fact, there could hardly be a better place to start, in this 'age of the self,' than the contrast between the Cartesian 'I am' (or rather, 'Am I?') and the 'I am' of Exodus 3:14. According to Owen Barfield, Coleridge's *Treatise on Logic* places 'I am' at the axis of all meaning. All the parts of speech, the elements of Grammar, subsist 'between the two poles of verb and noun, the one expressing activity and the other passivity, the one an action and the other a state.'[16] Thus Grammar revolves around an axis in which these two poles coincide: the verb *to be*, which 'expresses both action and state.' Only 'I am,' he says, is 'both verb and noun at the same time.' And of course 'I am' is the name God gives himself in the context of sending Moses to the sons of Israel.

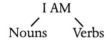

The *cogito* is supposed to represent a clear and distinct idea, a self-evident truth. The problem, in terms of the vision I am trying to develop in this book, is that Descartes did not begin with memory, with 'Grammar': he went straight to Thinking before going through Remembering. As Arthur Lovejoy explains, the road to philosophical idealism and subjectivism started when Descartes confined his reflection to the present moment, without observing that the self transcends the moment. *Memini ergo fui*: I remember, therefore I was. We cannot be conscious of the self if we are conscious *only* of the present moment. 'This is the primary mode of knowing, which must be presupposed, tacitly or explicitly, in any reflection upon the implications of what is sensibly given; and it is the kind of knowledge about the reality of which there is least disagreement.'[17]

Being, 'to be' (*esse*), is known in this remembering, which in the archetypal case of Moses is a summoning or a recalling to the

---

16 Owen Barfield, *Romanticism Comes of Age*, 153.
17 Arthur O. Lovejoy, *The Revolt Against Dualism*, 380.

feet of the one absolute 'I am,' the Source of language and thought and existence, and at the same time a 'sending' from there out into the world on a mission that defines who I *will be*. (I am what God gives me to do.)

In fact, as soon as Descartes starts to interpret or unpack his primary intuition, the problems appear. We notice, for example, that he immediately draws the conclusion that I am 'a substance which thinks,' quite distinct from my body in the material world. To the medieval mind, man (body and soul together) constitute a complete substance, but the soul is not complete in itself, and neither is the body.[18] The living body of a man is simply his soul made visible, the expression of a 'form' or principle of unity. That earlier understanding of man now has to be abandoned by Descartes—man is now supposed to be a composite of *two* substances, and it becomes exceedingly difficult to see how one of these substances can affect the other. It was much simpler for later philosophers to discard the notion of mind altogether—although idealists such as Berkeley found it more natural to discard the notion of matter. Either way, dualism collapsed into monism.[19]

In Search of Foundations

The problem the dialectician is faced with is sometimes called 'foundationalism.' How do we ground the basic principles of cor-

---

18 The medieval world had certainly been familiar with the notion of separated intellectual substances, but these were angels, not men. As Jacques Maritain pointed out, Descartes was trying to turn men into angels, albeit angels shackled to a body of matter.

19 The scepticism of Hume admitted only impressions or sensations and denied the notion of causality, on which Descartes had relied (along with the idea of God) to establish the existence of a material world. Kant tried to save time, space and causality by making them intuitions of the human mind. His so-called 'transcendental idealism' culminated in Hegel's notion of the Absolute Spirit and was deconstructed by Nietzsche. Thus each philosopher built on the mistakes, as well as the insights, of his predecessors. For some thoughts about the way Catholic phenomenologists have tried to retrieve a philosophy of Being, see Endnote 5.

rect thinking? Is there a common, neutral 'rationality' on which everyone can eventually agree? Education has been infected by this mood of uncertainty. Can we establish that there is one over-arching truth or 'reality' at all, or might there be a plurality of such truths depending on who observes them? Can we trust our sense-perceptions or might what we see be imposed on us by a deceptive spirit, or projected by our own consciousness? Must every event have a cause (and must the universe as a whole have a cause)? Why do scientists assume that the laws of nature are the same in all times and places? Am I confident that I exist—that the 'I' is a reality?

There is a sense in which all of these questions can be answered with a 'no.' But if so, can we teach anything other than the asking of questions (which, when no answers are forthcoming, will give way to the assertion of will and desire in an anarchy without respite)? We need to look more closely at the process of thinking if we are to 'save the Logos.' And when we do so, we realize that many of these foundational principles, as Chesterton indicated, are simply working assumptions. They are assumptions; but they work. They cannot be 'proved,' because they are too basic. But they cannot be doubted for very long without going mad. They are not so much principles we have discovered in the world, as rules by which we 'make sense' of the world. We choose to live as though the world made sense in this way, because it is better, more fulfilling, more rewarding, to do so than to live in an absurd world. In other words, reason is grounded on a communal act of faith.

There is, however, another way of looking at it. We have been searching for foundations, and the natural place to expect them is under our feet. But we have been looking in the wrong place. The foundations of reason, of 'Logic,' are over our heads. The world does not stand on them; it hangs from them, and in that literal sense 'depends' upon them. It is in this 'vertical' dimension that the universals exist. We don't have to prove their existence, as though they were just another kind of corporeal thing located in some mysterious region on the horizontal plane. If we look around us all we see are individual things, or parts of things. We have forgotten how to look, how to focus, in the other dimension—to see *through* things—where 'essences' reveal themselves.

John of Salisbury, in his *Metalogicon*, comes down heavily on the side of Aristotle against Plato in this argument about universals or essences. But there are in fact two kinds of universals which need to be distinguished. E. I. Watkin calls them 'abstract' and 'concrete' ideas. Plato's philosophy was much concerned with the latter, Aristotle's with the former. An *abstract* idea can be expressed by a clear definition, and is based on the discovery of what is common to some whole class of natural things. The various properties that are shared by 'cats' make them members of that species. A *concrete* idea, on the other hand, is the fullness and perfection of something, of which no particular example can be more than an approximation. That is to say, the concrete idea of a cat is the essence of 'catness' that I glimpse whenever I meet a cat. In this life, our knowledge of the concrete idea can only be somewhat obscure, but this is the inner form and the end or goal of the particular things I call by the name 'cat.' It is our intuition of the metaphysical basis for cats, and (in Christian terms) what God had in mind when he created them. A scientist needs to work with abstract ideas, because those can be defined in a clear and definite way, and subjected to measurement. But he also needs (and the poet certainly needs) the more obscure intuition of a concrete universal, which gives a sense of the underlying order of things.[20]

Evolution

In this light we can see a possible response to the challenge of evolutionary theory—the theory of evolution by natural selection which Pope John Paul II, in a famous address to the Pontifi-

---

20 E. I. Watkin, *A Philosophy of Form*, 112–19. This solution seems to echo one offered in the thirteenth century by St Albert the Great. For an attempt to untangle Plato from Aristotle's interpretation of him, see Giovanni Reale, *Toward a New Interpretation of Plato*. It is Christ who ties together the order of ideas and that of individuals, since as God he is the one all-inclusive 'concrete' idea (Logos), and as a man simply an individual.

cal Academy of Sciences,[21] called 'more than an hypothesis,' but which many Christians, even Catholics, consider an especially pernicious influence on modern thought and education.

Blessed John Paul II made his comment as part of a considered attempt to adjust the teaching of the *magisterium* to take account of recent scientific discoveries. Since the teaching of the Church does not 'change' though it does 'develop,' this meant detaching the essentials of the teaching from accidental accretions and less authoritative interpolations. A theory of evolution, he said, could be consistent with the Catholic faith about man provided it did not claim to derive spirit from matter, nor deny the 'ontological difference' that comes about when man becomes a 'spiritual soul' and a 'person' in direct relationship with God.

This leap to personhood is inherently mysterious, although we can guess roughly when it may have happened by observing that cave paintings and religious rituals seem to have begun around 30,000 years ago. But the Pope's statement did not tackle head-on the broader question of how one species evolves into another. He left that question to science, being concerned mainly to empha-size the direct creation of the human soul. We can address it— and at the same time help to explain the ontological leap made by the first men—by means of Watkin's distinction between 'abstract' and 'concrete' universals.

If *concrete ideas* of the various species or families of creatures do exist, the species we observe on earth do not have to be invented from below through a process of mutation and selection. Or rather, any transformation of that sort—in which we observe a succession of creatures 'morphing' from one type to another (if indeed such radical changes have been documented in the fossil record, which some still doubt)—can be explained in part by ref-erence to a process of 'vertical causation,' or the subtle influence of archetypes on the matter which they inform. It is, after all, a question of philosophy, and of whether our 'reason' will admit the existence of formal and final causes as a fundamentally differ-ent but valid kind of explanation, complementary to the material

21 Address to the Pontifical Academy of Sciences, 22 October 1996, avail-able at *www.newadvent.org/library/docs_jp02tc.htm*.

and efficient causes that have become the exclusive concern of modern science.[22]

The emergence of intelligent hominids, walking upright and conversing face to face, is no longer such a mystery if *all* species come about through a combination of vertical with horizontal types of cause.[23] But if we suppress the vertical dimension in creation altogether, reducing everything to a flux of energy, our very ability to think coherently, which depends on our ability to grasp the intelligible essences present in created things—the forms in the flux—will quickly disappear.

Dialectic

What I have been trying to suggest in this chapter is that one of the tasks of the Christian educator is to ground Thinking in Remembering, or Logic in Grammar, and to overcome the false Nominalism of our age with the spirit of contemplation.

As we saw, the specific body of methods that the Greeks developed for the training of thought—and the overcoming of sophistry by Philosophy—is called 'Dialectic.' In fact thinking is *dialogical* even before it is *logical*. We saw this when reflecting on the mythological account of the first Naming, which took place at the behest and in the presence of God. And indeed Adam's cry of joy and gratitude on seeing Eve as other than himself, a true partner in his loneliness, may be called the dawn of conscious thought. Thinking develops from this point; Philosophy is its elaboration, and Love its fruition.

---

22 See Etienne Gilson, *From Aristotle to Darwin and Back Again.*

23 The 'specialness' of humanity is not that a vertical influence is present in its creation, since that is the case with all animals and even plants. Rather, man's uniqueness lies in the fact that he is nothing less than the 'image and likeness' of God himself. In other words, the difference lies in the archetype, which in man's case is of a qualitatively different and higher order. I do not mean to imply, however, that evolution can be reduced to the inevitable unfolding or self-expression of *any* of these various archetypes without having a deeper foundation in the glorious freedom of God—see H. U. von Balthasar, *The Glory of the Lord,* vol. 5, 620–21.

And because thinking is dialogical, the best way to encourage it is by dialogue, debate, conversation. This is where the dialectical method, beginning with the Socratic *elenchus* in the early Platonic writings—a conversation designed to expose error—comes into its own. Plato's dialogues may seem at times to be rather artificial and unconvincing;[24] nevertheless, it can be a wonderful exercise to adapt them for performance with children as a way of stimulating them imaginatively to search for truth. Truth is not a quarry that can easily be pursued without the help of others, because our own thoughts have a tendency to run in circles. Our friends (in Adam's case, Eve) are given to us as 'helpers' in that quest, which leads ultimately to God.[25]

This theme will come more to the fore when we discuss Rhetoric or 'Speaking' in the next chapter, but already it has to be understood that learning, which is the expansion of the self, takes place in community. I am not referring only to the refinement of logical thought, which despite its importance is only a special case of thought in general, rendered more precise and coherent by the Principle of Contradiction, the Principle of Identity and Difference, and the Principle of the Excluded Middle, the details of which can be pursued elsewhere.[26] The development of thinking also involves the refinement of imagination and feeling.

The expansion of the self, we might say, requires the development of empathy and courtesy—empathy in order to be able to see another's point of view, and courtesy to act as though one were not the center of the world.

In fact, if the essence of something is best found in its highest

---

24 There is much disagreement about the value and purpose of the Socratic *elenchus*. The technique may in part have been intended to provoke and annoy, to create a 'shock' (like the shock from an electric eel) in those who thought they knew the truth, in order to render them more receptive. In the middle and later dialogues Plato seems to have favoured a gentler dialectical method.

25 There is a sense in which the truth, or God, lies at the center of the circle, but paradoxically it (or he) cannot be found there until discovered outside. We must love God with our whole heart, mind, and strength, and our neighbor as ourselves.

26 See Endnote 6.

or most perfect exemplar, then we might pay attention to Chesterton's remark that 'thanking is the highest form of thought,' especially as his insight is suggested by the etymology of the word itself. 'Thought' comes from the Old English *thanc* from which our word 'thank' is also derived. To *think* arises out of memory—which is, as we have seen, not simply the recalling of past events but the gathering and focusing of attention in the present. Thanking is the 'highest form of thought' because it penetrates to the highest truth about things: that they do not simply subsist in themselves but in another. Things that appear in my life subsist in a mysterious Other, but are given to me in such a way as to begin to subsist (to some degree) in me: they exist as 'gift,' and a gift is a call to give in return.

This must mean that to *thank* the Giver, the Origin, is to arrive at the ultimate truth of things, the truth that is sought in logical thought, the truth of what things are; for in their deepest nature things are expressions of the love that moves the stars.

Through Dialectic, or conversation, conducted in courtesy and thus in gratitude and respect, we ultimately arrive at the summit of human thought and discover that up there it is the same as prayer, or of that kind of prayer that is perfected in the liturgy of the Church. The word 'Eucharist' means 'thanksgiving,' and the *sacrifice of praise* that is the Catholic Mass or Divine Liturgy is nothing less than the joining together of man and God in the perfect act of giving and thanking. The Mass (and other forms of liturgical prayer) represent a kind of divinely-inspired Dialectic in the heart of the God-Man, in which we are privileged to participate. Liturgy is the consummation of education and the ultimate school of our humanity.

IV

Speaking

Rhetoric — Ethos — Community in the Real

The spirit receives two gifts simultaneously: the gift of knowing the truth and the gift of saying it. It would be unthinkable if it obtained only the first gift without the second. It would be burned up by an inward abundance that could not be expressed outwardly. It would be like a light that had to shine in itself without being able to emit any rays. . . . But from henceforth this revelation is free. Even though man is predisposed to communication in general, he is not compelled by nature to any one conscious communication in particular.[1]

THIS QUOTATION gives us the bridge we need from the theme of the previous chapter to this one. We are moving from the question of *how we know*, how we discover the truth by dialectics and logic, to *how we say or express* the truth to others, and how it radiates through us to them. Being capable of knowing the truth, we are capable also of speaking it, which is the concern of Rhetoric; although as we shall see, we can do so only in community and in freedom, as was also the case with Dialectic.

We recall also the earlier chapter on Grammar, or Remembering, the elements of which are presupposed both in this chapter and its predecessor. To know the truth we must first attend to reality. We must interpret reality. We must have names for things. We must 'remember Being.' And in fact Being itself is the first 'community' to which we belong: 'being' is itself a form of communion. That community comprises past, present, and future, to which we

---

1 Hans Urs von Balthasar, *Theo-Logic*, I, 93–4.

have access through memory, consciousness, and imagination. Initiation into a cultural and social *tradition* through education is the way in which we participate to the fullest in this community of being.

Word of God, Breath of God

We reveal ourselves by what we say and do not say. In God, the knowing (thinking) and the speaking are one with the self-gift that is the nature of the divine. The perfect Being is necessarily self-giving, self-communicating. The three persons of the Trinity are one God, one divine nature, perfectly given and shared: a community in love. Nothing else is necessary, nothing needs to exist in the same sense or the same degree as the three divine persons. But the *image* of that perfect self-giving and self-receiving cannot be quite as perfect as its archetype. In anything created, the gift of knowing and of saying can be distinguished, even separated. And the freedom of God, which coincides with perfect necessity, is reflected in a freedom that is not 'necessary' at all, and which requires at least a moment of deliberation and recollection.

Heart Speaks Unto Heart. This motto of the Blessed John Henry Newman, adopted from St Francis de Sales, contains the essence of a 'philosophy of communication,' which is also a philosophy of education. If education is about the communication of values, or meaningful information, and of wisdom and of tradition, between persons and across generations, it is important to know that it can only take place in the heart; that is, in the center of the human person. A voice from the lungs is not enough to carry another along with the meaning of our words. The voice has to carry with it the warmth and living fire of the heart around which the lungs are wrapped.[2]

Images of the heart as a place of fire, of the life-force, where the blood is warmed and energized, are found in all cultures and times. Human biology is more complex than this, but as simplifi-

2 The following expresses well the move from Grammar to Dialectic to Rhetoric: 'At the heart of a classical education is the word: the complete mastery of its shades of meaning, of its action-implicit imperatives, of its emotions and values. In ancient times such was the power of the word that it was believed to hold the key to the secrets of the external and internal realities.

cations go it is not a bad one. Each culture has worked out a more detailed physiological symbolism, but this will serve for the moment. The physical heart is the expression of an Idea; it corresponds to that in man which is both central and life-giving, or life-sustaining. This is the place where the breath comes from, and where it withdraws to. The heart mediates between the senses of the head (sight, hearing, smell, taste) and the feelings and needs of the stomach and lower organs. As the center of the organism, it is the place of our potential union with God—and God is secretly present there even for sinners. In Catholic devotion, the Sacred Heart of Jesus, crowned with flames, reminds us that God is a furnace of love in which all that is not compatible with love must eventually be consumed.

As has been mentioned already, the Logos exists entirely as dialogue (*dia-logos*). The Word is spoken on the breath of God (*ruah*, Spirit), God giving himself eternally, a perfect act of self-expression perfectly received and loved. Echoed in the Creation, this means that real human communication is only possible in the context of love, without which the self can neither be given in an act of speech (we describe someone as 'not meaning a word of it'), nor received in an act of sympathetic hearing (we accuse someone of 'not listening to what I was saying'). In fact every person has an interior life that cannot be divulged except by deliberately 'opening up' the heart, and allowing the life that is within it to flow through words and gestures into the other person.

Human speech flows from within, but if it is to serve the truth it cannot simply express what is within, and nothing else. Thought is an attempt to know; that is, a marriage of the self with reality; while speech is an attempt to bring about a meeting of selves, a communion in that marriage. Human speech and thought need to correspond with the order of the cosmos, the order of love.

The word, standing alone, was viewed as a microcosm of both *mythos* and *logos*, making life intelligible. God spoke the word, and out of nothing the object came into being. So in the classroom, the simple word *valor* and the fact that the teacher utters it with reverential passion might enliven the student's mind and through the imagination shape his character' (David V. Hicks, *Norms and Nobility*, 32).

Ethos

It is a question not simply of ethics, but of *ethos* (a word which in Greek is equivalent to 'character'). This topic belongs under the heading of 'Rhetoric' or 'Speaking' because in this section I am discussing the dimension of education that concerns interpersonal communication, or the creation and sustaining of a community and a tradition. Here what we *are* by our actions is the foundation of everything else. You cannot communicate a truth that has not changed you. You cannot *build a community* on a truth that has not been incorporated into you, making you the kind of person you are. The person is, to some extent, the message.

It would be an understatement to say that modern thinkers are divided on the major questions of ethics. But this poses an important challenge to teachers and educators. It seems hardly possible to teach morality in the schoolroom if philosophers themselves cannot agree about the very foundations of ethics. How do we respond to the great confusion in this area today? I don't think we need to despair. Postmodernism and relativism have had their day, and the basic outlines of an adequate framework for moral reflection have begun to emerge, not least through the work of John Paul II.

Ethics concerns what we should do or not do, and how we should behave. The new perspective developed by phenomenological realists and personalists in the twentieth century placed the 'acting person' at center stage, both in metaphysics (the study of what is), and in epistemology (the study of how and what we know).[3] The same is, of course, necessarily true in ethics, which is a reflection on human action in terms of intention and judgment. The new perspective is embodied in John Paul II's encyclical *Veritatis Splendor*), which Livio Melina introduces in this way:

> Morality can no longer be understood as a simple list of principles directing our choices and helping us to come to correct moral judgments. It is necessary to grasp the meaning of action and the way it implicates the acting subject. Thus, the

3 See Endnote 5.

very object of morality, now conceived within a larger and more comprehensive horizon, is redefined. It is no longer a question of 'what should I do?' as Kant had it, but rather of 'who am I called to be?'[4]

What I *am* is decided by my actions. What I do with my body not only reveals but determines who I am; it creates my destiny. But this destiny is not entirely arbitrary, not completely up to me. It is not that I can be whatever I choose. I have only two choices: I can either be, or fail to be, what God has created and called me to be.

In terms of education, this means that the best way to communicate morality is not through endless dry lists of what should and should not be done, but once again through the imagination— through stories, drama, and living examples capable of engaging the will and the emotions and thus inspiring us to be better people. A morality, an *ethos*, must be embodied; it must be lived by a human being, before it can be understood or communicated. It is expressed in the virtues that are the powers by which we build character, and with the fruits of those virtues, which manifest the growing presence of the Holy Spirit in our lives—twelve fruits, to be precise, which we see demonstrated in the lives of the saints, and which could be called the criteria of sanctity: peace, joy, love, faithfulness, gentleness, generosity, patience, kindness, goodness, modesty, self-control, and chastity.[5]

Who Am I, Again?

The modern confusion among professional philosophers means that we feel unable to assert or affirm an ethical perspective for fear of being accused of trying to impose our religious beliefs. But this is because ethics has been reduced to a squabble over

4 Livio Melina, *The Epiphany of Love*, xv.

5 Chastity, of course, is not the same as virginity or abstinence, but means something more like 'purity' and is required of the married as well as the single. See my booklet, *The Fruits of the Spirit*, online at http://thechristianmysteries.blogspot.com, for detailed study of the Fruits and their relationship to the various virtues.

lists of principles, of do's and don'ts, in the absence of any shared belief in an 'end' or 'form' of human nature. If there is no goal, appointed by God or nature, then by default we each have to make one up or decide it for ourselves, often on the basis of whatever desires happen to be uppermost in our minds. We choose for ourselves, and negotiate our principles and rules of conduct in view of the pragmatic goal we have set ourselves.

If actions have no interior meaning of their own (no reference, that is, to an order of ideas or 'universals'), but only a subjective meaning given them by the goal to which they happen to be directed by the human will, then my acts are entirely justified or not by their intended consequences. An evil act might be done for a 'good' end; in fact, in certain circumstances it would cease to be 'evil' at all. If this were the case, a policeman might consent to torturing a child in order to avoid blowing his cover with some group of criminals he is trying to bring to justice. But actions do have a meaning, aside from their consequences, intended or not. This follows from the nature of human actions as the expressions of the self, the person.

To shoot someone in cold blood because I don't like him is one kind of act; to shoot an enemy under orders during a legitimate war is another. The reason for which I do something is certainly important. But to the extent that I know *what it is* that I am doing to achieve that end, the 'what' is just as important as the reason I am doing it.

In one of the Endnotes to this book (Endnote 5), I discuss the overcoming of Cartesian dualism by means of a phenomenology of action, or the acting person. In his encyclical about ethics, *Veritatis Splendor*, Pope John Paul II writes,

> The reason why a good intention is not itself sufficient, but a correct choice of actions is also needed, is that the human act depends on its object, whether that object is *capable or not of being ordered* to God, to the One who 'alone is good,' and thus brings about the perfection of the person. An act is therefore good if its object is in conformity with the good of the person. (VS, 78)

If acts are intrinsically evil, a good intention or particular circumstances can diminish their evil, but they cannot remove it. They remain 'irremediably' evil acts; *per se* and in themselves they are not capable of being ordered to God and to the good of the person. (VS, 81)

Certain acts may not be done even in order to bring about a good result, because to do them is to commit a sin. The act itself, in this case, cannot be 'ordered' to God. The Pope reaffirms a list of such 'intrinsically evil acts' given by the Council:

Whatever is hostile to life itself, such as any kind of homicide, genocide, abortion, euthanasia and voluntary suicide; whatever violates the integrity of the human person, such as mutilation, physical and mental torture and attempts to coerce the spirit; whatever is offensive to human dignity, such as subhuman living conditions, arbitrary imprisonment, deportation, slavery, prostitution and trafficking in women and children; degrading conditions of work which treat labourers as mere instruments of profit, and not as free responsible persons: all these and the like are a disgrace, and so long as they infect human civilization they contaminate those who inflict them more than those who suffer injustice, and they are a negation of the honor due to the Creator. (VS, 80)

To summarize what was said earlier, if asked who I am, I might reply, *I am what I do.* This implies that I make myself what I am by acting in a certain way. Our Catholic ethics is an ethics of virtue—of acting not just in order to bring about certain results, but of acting in order to correspond to the Good, which is not at all the same thing. In fact we can go further, and say, I am what I do *to others.* This connects us with the Golden Rule: *Do unto others as you would have them do unto you.*

I should not perform any action that is unworthy of a human person. This notion of the ethical self-in-action can be extended further by reference to the concept of vocation. Each of us is called not just to goodness, but to holiness. This was one of the teachings of the Second Vatican Council (*Lumen Gentium*,

Chapter 5). Holiness is sanctification; it is unity with God. The cosmos itself is not complete, it does not achieve its end in God, until humanity through the use of its freedom attains this unity, this holiness. This goes for each of us. You and I have an end in God, a goal to which God is calling us and for which he created us. That is the 'saint' we must strive to become. We become this true, fulfilled, and happy self—our self in God—by fulfilling the mission, the purpose, for which we were sent into the world. Thus on a deeper level I am not just what I happen to do, or choose to do; I am that which God *gives me to do* (see pages 75–76). I am my mission.[6]

Recovery of Freedom

We must not lose sight of how radical this is. John Paul writes, citing St Paul (Eph. 5:8–11, 15–16; 1 Th. 5:4–8):

> It is urgent then that Christians should rediscover *the new-ness of the faith and its power to judge* a prevalent and all-intrusive culture. As the Apostle Paul admonishes us: 'Once you were darkness, but now you are light in the Lord; walk as children of the light (for the fruit of the light is found in all that is good and right and true), and try to learn what is pleasing to the Lord. Take no part in the unfruitful words of darkness, but instead expose them. . . . Look carefully then how you walk, not as unwise men but as wise, making the most of the time, because the days are evil.' (VS, 88)

Even Christians tend to assume that morality is a matter of adhering to a set of rules and thereby becoming better people. But the 'norm' of Christian action is not a set of rules, not even the 'natural law.' It is Christ. He is the way, the truth and the life.

---

6 In the theology of Balthasar, one might even say that the person is *defined* in terms of mission, beginning with the second Person of the Trinity, whose mission is to do the will of the One who sent him. One's true 'mission,' of course, and the degree to which one managed to fulfil it, may not become apparent until the afterlife, when one sees everything as God sees it.

This is the ultimate implication of adopting the perspective of 'the acting person.'[7]

There is a kind of paradox here. Christian morality is the opposite of selfish, and yet it forbids me to do anything incompatible with my eternal salvation, even if doing so would materially help another person. The reason is that such an action (the kinds of actions described above as intrinsically evil) will inevitably bring about greater evil than the good I am tempted to seek. In that sense, consequentialism is not entirely false. The consequences *are* important. But no human being can know all the consequences of any action. I cannot decide to act entirely on that basis—I have to take account of the nature of the action itself, as it exists in the present.

This is the key to a Catholic morality. The Pope describes it as the inseparable connection between freedom and truth, for 'only the freedom which submits to the Truth leads the human person to his true good. The good of the person is to be in the Truth and to do the Truth' (VS, 84).

The modern mistake about freedom, which a Catholic education should root out and destroy, is that freedom has nothing to do with truth. We imagine that the more choices we have, the freer we are. In reality, a multitude of choices makes us no freer than we were before unless we have the freedom (that is, the power, the ability) to choose between the right action and the wrong action. Thus the truth about good and evil is intimately bound up with our freedom. It is the quality not the quantity of our choices that counts. A myriad of evil choices is no choice at all. Aquinas writes: 'Liberty or free will does not essentially consist in the power of choosing between good and evil. All that is required is the power to choose, without being forced by necessity, one particular good rather than another. To possess the power to choose evil is a sign not of perfection but of weakness' (ST, 1a, q. 62, art. 8).[8]

There are commandments inscribed in the human heart,

---

7 See S. Pinckaers OP, *Morality: The Catholic View*; H. Schurmann et al., *Principles of Christian Morality*; C. Caffara, *Living in Christ*.

8 See also Endnote 7.

which we know collectively as the natural law. These are not the arbitrary decisions of an extrinsic divine lawgiver. They are the consequences of the fact we can find *fulfilment* only in certain ways and not others. The 'thou shalt nots' are the results and corollaries of something more fundamental to our nature: the single positive commandment, 'thou shalt love.' And the picture of this positive is completed for us when the Ten Commandments are supplemented by the Beatitudes of Christ in the Sermon on the Mount, his fleshed-out description of the human calling, which is also a kind of self-portrait.

This is what it means to 'do' the Truth. In Christ we see the beauty that our heart wants to live. This is the key to a Catholic 'liberal' education—an education for freedom.

Poetic Form

On this basis we can at last understand the essence of Rhetoric— which is not a set of techniques to impress (oratory, eloquence),[9] nor a means of manipulating the will and emotions of others (sophistry, advertising), but rather a way of liberating the freedom of others by showing them the truth in a form they can understand.[10]

A form they can understand, because (as we saw with Hugh of St Victor), rhetoric is 'the discipline of persuading to every suitable thing,' and no one is persuaded of something they do not feel

9 From the time of Cicero onwards, the rules of eloquence involved at least five techniques: the collection, arrangement and verbal expression of the materials, memorization of the speech and the art of delivery in one of three styles: plain, moderate or grand. Of course, all of these techniques can be misused.

10 The original 'sophists' seem to have been a school or movement of rhetoricians originating in Sicily at the end of the fifth century BC. As mentioned earlier they were often more interested in the arts of persuasion than in uncovering truth. (See Sister Miriam Joseph CSC, *The Trivium*, 225, and also Plato, *Sophist*.) After reform by Isocrates, a contemporary of Socrates, the rhetorical tradition of the sophists became a more moral enterprise, and was later picked up by the Roman orators and developed into a broad curriculum of studies. This was one of the influences on the later liberal arts tradition (see Endnote 1).

they understand. We may understand only dimly, or 'as in a mirror,' but if we are to *follow with our own will* we must recognize in that thing some good and some truth that we need for our own fulfilment in life.

In order to 'persuade' in this sense, and to do so 'efficiently,' a speaker's words must be 'charged with meaning to the utmost possible degree,' as Ezra Pound said of great literature.[11] This turns out to be much the same as the characteristic of beauty identified by Aquinas as *claritas* (clarity, clearness, shiningness), which refers to the transparency of a thing to the *form* that dwells within it and makes it what it is.

This is one of many reasons why it is such a shame to deprive children of exposure to the greatest writers in the English language. In the great writers one can see how words are charged with meaning. In the essay just referred to, Pound claims that language is especially charged or energized in three ways:

MELOPOEIA, wherein the words are charged, over and above their plain meaning, with some musical property, which directs the bearing or trend of that meaning.

PHANOPOEIA, which is a casting of images upon the visual imagination.

LOGOPOEIA, 'the dance of the intellect among words,' that is to say, it employs words not only for their direct meaning, but it takes count in a special way of habits of usage, of the context we *expect* to find with the word, its usual concomitants, of its known acceptances, and of ironical play. It holds the aesthetic content which is peculiarly the domain of verbal manifestation, and cannot possibly be contained in plastic or in music. It is the latest come, and perhaps most tricky and undependable mode.

For the most intense experience of language, all three of these properties will be present—music, imagery, and connotation. I want to draw attention especially to the first of these. In his interesting and influential essay on *English Metrical Law,* the Victorian

---

11 Ezra Pound, 'How to Read,' in *New York Herald Tribune Books,* 1929.

poet and essayist Coventry Patmore explains the musical quality that good prose has in common with good poetry in terms of 'harmonious numbers' and specifically rhythm. (Flaubert is famously said to have worked out a rhythm for the final pages of *Madame Bovary* before coming up with the words.) Rhythm or metre is a mathematical structure, a structure of repetition and variation. It creates a shape in time, a dynamic flowing movement that carries the mind along with it. If prose lacks rhythm, it leaves us behind. Our attention is too easily diverted from the direction in which the author intends us to move. Something similar is true of all art, from music through to architecture and even painting, which, although seemingly static, requires us to move our attention through time in order to absorb it. (A painting that can be appreciated entirely at a single glance, without leaving something further to explore, is probably not a very good painting.)

This insight into the musical nature of all speech, especially poetry, and the refusal to draw any clear lines between poetry and prose, lies close to the heart of Patmore's argument in this essay. He is part of an ancient tradition, summarized by Jacques Maritain as the idea that poetry 'is the secret life of each and all of the arts; another name for what Plato called *mousikè*.' Poetry is here defined as that 'intercommunication between the inner being of things and the inner being of the human Self which is a kind of divination' (a discerning of meaning).[12]

Although Patmore defends precise rules of versification, he also argues that the best poetry does not follow the rules tamely and as if mechanically, but will convey *feeling* by constant little tensions with the underlying structure, little departures from the standard pattern. (The same is true in music. It must constantly surprise us in little ways; which it can only do if the form to which it basically conforms creates a framework of expectation.) Thus 'there seems to be a perpetual conflict between the law of the verse and freedom of the language, and each is incessantly, though insignificantly, violated for the purpose of giving effect to the other.'

12 Jacques Maritain, *Creative Intuition in Art and Poetry*, 3.

Patmore believed that music and metre 'is as natural to spoken language as an even pace is natural to walking.' Just as 'dancing is no more than an increase of the element of measure which already exists in walking, so verse is but an additional degree of that metre which is inherent in prose speaking.' From there he returns to the theme of music in poetry—what pleases us in verse, he says, is not merely *rhythm*, in the sense of a measured beat, but 'rhythmical *melody*'; not *monotones* like the ticking of a clock or the pulsing of a chime, but the repetition of sounds in which can be heard (or imagined) a variety of tones. The very highest form of verse therefore coincides with the highest form of human speech, namely *song*, where all these factors are combined along with the ideas and images that may be suggested in words.[13]

Rhetoric, in the sense I want to give it here—the art of communication—is in this view intimately related to poetry, dance, and song. We might even conclude that the best way to teach it is in close connection with these. In other words, an ability to communicate in words will grow with a sense of rhythm, timing, melody, and physical grace. But why should we ever have thought otherwise? Communication in the fullest sense must involve the whole person, that is body, soul, and spirit, with imagination and intellect in harmony. Rhetoric cannot be kept entirely separate from any other subject, least of all those which cultivate our sense of beauty. The interconnectedness of things— their mutual indwelling and transparency—is the condition of communication. All words need the Word, the Logos in which they cohere and on which they stand.

Thus we have George Steiner's point 'that any coherent under-

---

13 The final section of his essay distinguishes the three great classes of English poetry: alliterative, rhyming, and rhymeless or 'blank' verse. Rhyme is 'the great means, in modern languages, of marking essential metrical pauses.' Alliteration, or the repetition of consonants, which is the basis of Anglo-Saxon poetry, is also a way of marking the metre by 'conferring emphasis on the accent.' He defends and explains the important role of alliteration, cunningly used even in modern verse to enhance the impression of metre 'as if by magic,' and also the use of rhyme against its critics (such as Thomas Campion), before finally discussing the metres used in blank verse.

standing of what language is and how language performs, that any coherent account of the capacity of human speech to communicate meaning and feeling is, in the final analysis, underwritten by the assumption of God's presence.' He adds:

> This study will contend that the wager on the meaning of meaning, on the potential of insight and response when one human voice addresses another, when we come face to face with the text and work of art or music, which is to say when we encounter the *other* in its condition of freedom, is a wager on transcendence.[14]

We make the same wager here.

The Liturgical Heart

For that reason, the final section of this chapter on Rhetoric will be concerned with liturgy, or with the 'liturgical consummation' of education and of the Trivium.

The public and shared act of worship, especially the Mass, is where we learn the *ethos* of a Catholic culture. Faith, reason, and imagination come together in liturgy. A school without a liturgy, like a culture or civilization similarly deprived, is cut off from the source of its unity and its life. It may survive for a generation or two, using up the spiritual capital of the past, but it will wither and decline eventually.[15] This has been hinted at in the documents published by the Congregation of Religious Education, but has not received enough attention in Catholic writings about

---

14 George Steiner, *Real Presences*, 4.

15 This Chestertonian intuition is given some substance by the historian Christopher Dawson, for whom 'spiritual alienation of its own greatest minds is the price that every civilization has to pay when it loses its religious foundations, and is contented with a purely material success. We are only just beginning to understand how intimately and profoundly the vitality of a society is bound up with its religion. It is the religious impulse which supplies the cohesive force which unifies a society and a culture. The great civilizations of the world do not produce the great religions as a kind of cultural by-product; in a very real sense the great religions are the foundations on which the great civilizations rest' (*Progress and Religion*, 232–3).

education generally. Even among Catholic educators, the liturgy tends to be regarded as an add-on or a necessary 'marker' of the Catholic identity of a school, but little more. The difficulty of persuading the majority of pupils to take it seriously or even to attend is something teachers and administrators are all too aware of, and there are no easy solutions to this.

We can glean the importance of the question by looking at an interesting document from the Vatican's Congregation for Catholic Education in 2007, *Educating Together in Catholic Schools*. Though concerned primarily with the shared mission between consecrated persons and the lay faithful, the core of the document was an exposition of the personalist philosophy applied to education. This it formulates as follows:

> Every human being is called to communion because of his nature which is created in the image and likeness of God (cf. Gen. 1:26–27). Therefore, within the sphere of biblical anthropology, man is not an isolated individual, but a *person*: a being who is essentially relational. The communion to which man is called always involves a double dimension, that is to say vertical (communion with God) and horizontal (communion with people). It is fundamental that communion be acknowledged as a gift of God, as the fruit of the divine initiative fulfilled in the Easter mystery.[16]

Communion, the document states, is 'the "essence" of the Church, the foundation and source of its mission of being in the world,' and this communion comes about in and through Christ; for 'communion with the Trinity rendered possible by the encounter with Christ,' the document states, is what 'unites persons with one other.'[17] The document therefore presents a

---

16 Congregation for Catholic Education, 'Educating Together in Catholic Schools: A Shared Mission Between Consecrated Persons and the Lay Faithful' (2007), section 8. In section 44 the Congregation states: 'The human being, as a person, is a unity of soul and body that is dynamically realized through its opening to a relation with others. A person is formed for *being-with* and *for-others*, which is realized in love.'

17 Ibid., sections 9 and 10.

strongly person-centered vision of the school as a place of communion. Unfortunately, rather than focus immediately on the foundational importance of prayer and the liturgy in the creation and maintenance of this communion, the document goes on to talk about community and the 'spirit of communion,' rather vaguely defined, before mentioning almost in passing that 'ecclesial maturity' must be 'nourished by the encounter with Christ in the sacraments.'[18]

I cannot help feeling that—despite nods to the importance of prayer and holiness of life nourished by the sacraments—something vital has been missed here. The emphasis on communion and personal relations is important, but it needs to be fleshed out. Compare this excellent formulation from the educational plan of a school in Washington, DC:

> Religion is not just one subject within the curriculum, but the key to its unity and integration. The cosmos is an ordered, unified whole because it is created in Christ—'in whom all things hold together' (Col. 1:17). Belief in God as our Father and the world as His beautiful and rational creation binds faith and reason, nature and culture, art and science, morality and reality into a coherent and integrated unity. This unified view reaches its summit in worship, which is the highest form of knowledge and thus the end and goal of true education.[19]

If this is the case (as I have argued also in *Beauty for Truth's Sake*), then we need to rethink the way that prayer and the Mass are presented in our schools, and integrated into the curriculum—bearing in mind, of course, the presence within the school of some who have no active faith and others who may belong to different traditions of worship and belief entirely.

Communion, the Congregation for Divine Worship affirmed, is a 'gift of God' and 'fruit of the divine initiative' fulfilled at

---

18 Ibid., section 17.
19 *The Educational Plan of St Jerome Classical School* (2010), 11. Published online under 'Classical Education' at *www.stjeromes.org/stjeromeschool. htm.*

Easter. That initiative reaches us in the sacraments, especially Baptism and the Eucharist. Thus the document itself implies that the communion of the school originates in the Mass. But how might we implement this insight within the school?

There are three main ways, which I will call *Mystagogy, Integration,* and *Example.*

Mystagogy refers to the missing or underplayed element in most contemporary catechesis, namely the explanation and exploration of the symbolic meanings and theological dimension of the rites of the Church—and not just the rites but the gestures, words, music, images, and structures associated with those rites. It is all too easy, especially when the liturgy is simplified and rendered banal in a misguided attempt to make it more easily intelligible, to become bored and indifferent during Mass. Energetic children, whose attention span is very short, suffer from this problem intensely, as every parent knows. Teenagers who think they have 'understood' the Mass and 'heard it all before' have another set of difficulties.

It is certainly not possible to turn the Mass into an entertainment to compete with the secular attractions available outside.[20] (This has been tried, and the contemporary 'reform of the reform' and the 2007 papal *motu proprio* lifting restrictions on the Extraordinary Form of the Mass was partly a reaction to these excesses.) But what might be possible is to communicate something of the true nature of the Mass, taking it out of the category of entertainment altogether so that it does not have to compete. Such a catechesis might focus on ideas such as the following:

- The Mass takes place in sacred time: it is a kind of time-machine that overcomes the boundaries between past, present, and future.
- The Mass is a personal encounter with the Invisible—with Jesus Christ risen from the dead.
- The Mass is a marriage, a consummation of the relation-

---

20 In any case, one of the good fruits of being obliged to attend a boring ceremony on a regular basis, provided one can avoid the build-up of resentment, is a certain mastery of one's own energies and an ability to focus one's attention on one thing for a longer period of time.

ship between God and Man, between Christ and his Church.

• Every Mass is different because we bring different experiences and concerns to it each day.

• The Mass comes alive when it is used as a prayer. This means it requires to be filled with our own attention, our own self-gift, moment by moment.

• Our own interior offering is supposed to be made at the same time and as part of the priest's offertory. This makes us, too, 'priests' in a sense—priests of creation.

• The Mass is cosmic: it connects every part and element and dimension of the universe. This fact is reflected in the liturgical seasons and vestments.

• The Mass is constructed in symbolic code, drawn partly from Scripture. In fact it offers a way to discover the inner meaning of the Bible.

• Every element of the Mass, every gesture made by the priest or ourselves, as well as the way we arrange the space and the furnishings of the church, not to mention the images we use, has a variety of meanings (moral, historical, mystical, etc.).

I have been speaking of the Mass, but a mystagogical approach can also be applied to the Divine Office and the rest of the Church's prayers, including the Stations of the Cross and the Rosary.

The kind of continuing catechesis I have in mind is not mere intellectual explanation, but an ongoing initiation into prayer and the interior dimensions of Catholic practice. Teenagers tend to drop away from the Church when this kind of formation has been lacking in their lives. Furthermore prayer is a universal experience, and many Catholic devotions are echoed and shared by other religious traditions. Formation in prayer and the cultivation of the 'religious sense' is something that should not be reserved only for Catholics within the school, even if not everyone can participate in the sacraments.

Integration. The second way to restore the liturgy to a central place is by *integrating* it with everything else that is being taught—not crudely or simplistically, of course, but by tracing the points of connection between things that exist in reality. If God the Creator and Redeemer is genuinely the center of all things, there will be indications in all things that point to him. We need to be attentive to these, and to look deeply enough to see them. We may also need to exercise considerable patience. Not everything can be discovered or accounted for at once.

The notion of 'drama' is particularly helpful as a way of integrating human knowledge—and it dovetails with the central emphasis we want to give to the human person in a Catholic school. The term 'person' derives from the ancient word for a theatrical mask (*persona*) representing the character an actor was portraying on stage; this was transformed and deepened by Christianity as a way of speaking about identity-in-relation, first in God (Father, Son, Spirit) and secondly among men.

A drama is a story that unfolds in a given context between several characters—each human life can be viewed as such a story, as can the history of mankind as a whole. Cosmology, astronomy, and geography give us the stage and the set and the props, while history and psychology and religion give us the plot and the action. Everything makes sense, everything connects, through the person whose character, actions, and destiny are the subject of the story.

In this way, the study of the Bible can be transformed (as it is by reading Scripture through the liturgy). Too often children see the Bible as a seemingly interminable rag-bag collection of stories, like that of Adam and Eve, Noah and the Ark, or the Parables of Jesus, interspersed with 'boring bits' about genealogies and a great deal of obscure prophetic ranting. But once we see the Bible as organized around the unfolding drama between God and Israel, culminating in our own baptism and reception of the Eucharist, the mystery of Scripture begins to reveal itself. The unity of the narrative provides a key to the meaning of our own lives as players on a world stage.

In relation to the drama of God revealing himself to man, and eventually as man, the rest of world history can also be connected to our own lives. The search for God in other religions makes more sense once we have seen the way God searches for man in the Bible. The great religions provide the inspiration and impetus for the arts and sciences. The emergence of modern atheism is seen against the background of the search for truth, as a reaction to distortions of faith.

By teaching Scripture alongside modern science, with perfect respect for reason as well as faith, the point is made from the very outset that faith and reason are complementary. Like the capstone of an arch, faith enables the elements established by reason to stand and balance against each other, forming a structure in which they all make sense. A child will not at first notice any disparity between the story of the Garden of Eden and that of the Big Bang and the evolution of the dinosaurs, but by being told that both are true he is protected from slipping at a later stage into an overly literalistic approach to the Bible.

In a Catholic school, it is not the Bible that is central, but the liturgy. The Bible is read through the lens of the liturgy. That is to say, the unity of the Bible (made up as it is of diverse fragments and genres, composed over millennia) lies just beyond the surface of the text, in the figure of Christ who is encountered by us in the liturgy. Our faith enables us to see in the Eucharist the same Christ whom the disciples encountered and the prophets glimpsed. Once kindled, that faith can illuminate the whole of our existence, along with the manifold relationships that define our existence.

Example. The third way to give the liturgy a central place is, of course, by living it. Clearly not every teacher or pupil will be equally devout. Not all will have a living faith. But there must be some whose example demonstrates that devotion is possible. It only takes one, but it is better if there is a community of such disciples. In the person who has encountered Christ and is living with him, the rest of us can see not only that Christianity is possible, but that Christ exists and lives in others.

What is glimpsed in the life of a true follower of Jesus—one whose existence is centered on prayer and the sacraments—is a substantiality, a solidity, a quality of reality, that makes any other way of life seem less real, less complete, more unsatisfactory. It corresponds to something I may only be obscurely aware of in myself, namely a hunger for infinity. Human desire is not like animal desire, because unlike a purely biological instinct ours cannot, in the end, be satisfied by anything less than God. That is why we can make such a mess of the world: once diverted away from their true object, our passions run rampant and are limited only by the physical limits of creation (which through technology we then seek to expand).

It is one of the great teachers of modern times, Luigi Giussani (the founder of Communion and Liberation, which grew from a small movement in the Italian high schools and universities to a worldwide cultural phenomenon involving many hundreds of thousands of young people), who used to say that we can only communicate a truth that has changed us. That is why we need the sacraments. In the sacraments we do not simply read about Christ or learn about him, but are touched by him, and changed.

> The Eucharist is not only Christ's act but is also 'mine,' and my act is identified with that of Christ, who in turn identifies his with mine. The Offertory is my own gesture, and so is the Consecration, and the Communion consummates and completes this act of mine. Our sacrifice coincides with the offer we make of our self which is implied in the recognition that Christ is our entire self, as we accept him and try to act in accordance with this awareness. . . .[21]

This brings us back to what was said in the second chapter about the quality of loving attention, and the presence of the 'third'—the Spirit—in the relationship between pupil and teacher. In the Mass, in the Eucharist, all the relationships that make up the school—between pupils, between teachers, between teachers and students—are gathered into the great archetypal sacrifice that takes away our sins and gives us new life. The true Head of the school becomes visible. The Spirit of the school becomes manifest. Those for whom faith has not yet become a reality, or those of other faiths who are part of the same community of the school, need not be witnesses to this event, for by its nature it can be seen only by the eyes of faith. It suffices that they benefit from the presence of the Spirit, who is known less by

---

21 *The Risk of Education: Discovering Our Ultimate Destiny,* 43.

preaching than by example and by genuine friendship—attention to each other in love.

In this chapter we have been concerned with the foundations of Rhetoric. In order to reach those foundations I had to discuss ethics, personal identity, and the nature of freedom, as well as how we give a 'poetic form' to language that can reach from heart to heart. But we discovered that the meaningfulness of our speech ultimately depends on our making a 'wager on transcendence,' and so we come back to the point that the whole educational process, and Rhetoric in particular, comes to a head and reaches some kind of 'consummation' in the liturgical act, the act of worship. We all knew that the Mass must be important in a Catholic school, but perhaps now we can see more clearly that it is not just a necessary point of reference, but intrinsic to the educational process itself.

V

Wisdom

Beyond the Liberal Arts

Of all things to be sought, the first is that Wisdom in which the Form of the Perfect Good stands fixed.[1]

WE HAVE SEEN that the liberal arts are deeply entangled with the metaphysical tradition of the West, which goes back to the Greeks, but they also borrow a great deal from the Wisdom tradition of ancient Israel.[2] In a very real sense it is a case of 'Athens meeting Jerusalem'; indeed, 'marrying' Jerusalem might be more apt.

The Trivium represents the first or foundational stage of the liberal arts, understood broadly as an education in freedom. (By calling it 'foundational' I do not mean to imply that it is left behind in the later stages of education.) It gives us grounding for greater freedom and responsibility in three ways, by developing our ability to imagine, think, and communicate. The child needs to grow in these three dimensions to be fully integrated with society. If any of the three are lacking he will be cut off from society and become an isolated and rather lonely particle, frenetic or depressed; one lost fragment of a broken puzzle.

But how do we begin to move from these very theoretical statements towards some kind of implementation in a school or syllabus? And are we not in danger of leaving out some vitally important elements?

1 *The* Didascalicon *of Hugh of Saint Victor*, 46.
2 See Endnotes 1 and 8.

Hugh of St Victor, writing in the Boethian and Augustinian tradition in the late 1130s (the author of the quote that stands at the head of the present chapter), had a very broad understanding of the purpose of education. It was nothing less than the pursuit of Wisdom; and so he gave to it the overall title of 'Philosophy' (the word itself meaning 'love of wisdom'). He quotes Boethius as saying: 'Philosophy is the love of that Wisdom which, wanting in nothing, is a living Mind and the sole primordial Idea or Pattern of things.'[3] Thus education is all about Philosophy, and Philosophy is divided into four main branches of knowledge, these being the theoretical arts or sciences (striving for the contemplation of truth in, supremely, theology), the practical (for the regulation of society through morality, economics, and politics), the mechanical (for the occupations of this life, including commerce, medicine, fabric-making, theatre, etc.), and the logical (for correct speaking and clear argumentation).[4] Within this scheme it is what he terms the logical that has been the main concern of this book, because it comprises the arts of language or the Trivium.

Although Hugh then goes on to emphasize the importance of seven of these arts (under the headings of the Trivium and Quadrivium), he does so because the ancients considered them 'so to excel all the rest in usefulness that anyone who had been thoroughly schooled in them might afterward come to a knowledge of the others by his own inquiry and effort rather than by listening to a teacher.'[5] In other words, the importance of the

3 The Didascalicon of Hugh of Saint Victor, 61.

4 There are naturally many ways of dividing things up, each of which may have merit. For example, Kenneth L. Schmitz also speaks of *four* primary disciplines, or elemental ways of talking about things (a good 'Pythagorean' number of which Hugh would have approved). 'They are four fundamental modes of discourse, four basic ways of giving a rational account of things, four paths to understanding them' (The Recovery of Wonder, 17–24). They are philosophy, mathematics, history, and linguistics (studying respectively being, number, time, and the word). These are the paths that Western civilization took, beginning in myth, to achieve eventually a certain objectifying 'distance' from the world, giving a new power over it, but amounting in the end, after various twists and turns, to a kind of alienation.

5 The Didascalicon of Hugh of Saint Victor, 86–7.

other studies was not disputed, but they were regarded as less demanding and requiring a less intense educational effort.

The Other Arts

I have mentioned the wider picture because I am concerned that what I have said so far may appear to suggest a rather restricted notion of the topics and methods a Catholic education should embrace. For example, in the early liberal arts tradition, what we would call 'arts' or 'fine arts' (apart from music theory) were often deliberately excluded, being relegated to the category of 'servile.' These were arts or skills that had an immediate practical purpose; namely, to equip one for a vocation among the lower classes of society. But to a large extent, Christianity has gradually undermined this distinction between liberal and servile. The Benedictine Order, in particular, contributed to the revolution by mixing manual with intellectual labor in the life of a monk, and subordinating both to prayer. The three were no longer to be kept separate, for Christian anthropology implied a unity-in-distinction between body, soul, and spirit. The unity in question is that of the human person, who is not a soul temporarily lumbered with a body but a spiritual-corporeal whole, possessing as such an eternal destiny. Nor do we today accept the class distinctions that were universal in the ancient world (in part because the development of technology has freed the wealthy from dependence upon a caste of servants).

In any attempt to draw inspiration from the Trivium for education today, therefore, it is necessary to open up our conception of the three 'ways' quite considerably, if they are to serve as the foundations for a broad modern education. I have begun to do this not only by applying them to the early stages of education rather than to university courses, but also by deepening the very categories themselves. I have also hinted how Remembering, Thinking, and Speaking are related to—and might even be said to encompass—the fine arts as well. Grammar, Dialectic, and Rhetoric have been roughly associated with the Persons of the Trinity in the order Father, Son, and Holy Spirit, as well as with Memory, Thought, and Speech, and similarly with *Mythos*, *Logos*, and *Ethos* respectively. If we are to find a place for the fine arts, too, it seems to me that the best way to do so is to associate Grammar with music and dance, Dialectic with the visual and plastic arts, and Rhetoric with drama. Let me make the reasons for this slightly more explicit.

The Trivium as such is concerned with the arts of language. But the other arts are also 'expressive'—not merely decorative or practical. Indeed we often talk about the 'language' of painting or architecture, or of a particular artist. The visual arts may serve as a support for spiritual contemplation every bit as much as a work of philosophy or theology.[6]

The arts of music and dance are arts of movement, arts that unfold over time, and for this reason I have associated them with the Father, as the prime mover of all things, and with the 'memory of being' which we have identified with Grammar, concerned with the root-structures of language and self-awareness. They lead us by way of sound and movement back to the silence and stillness that is the origin of all things.

The visual and plastic arts (painting, iconography, architecture, sculpture) are arts of the image. As such I tend to associate them with the Son, the image or Icon of the Father, on whose body our very churches are modeled. When the iconoclasts of Byzantium were defeated at the Seventh Ecumenical Council and icons were reinstated, the making (or 'writing') of images was not only encouraged but sanctified. When Moses spoke to the Lord and reported his words to the people, his face shone so brightly that they were afraid to approach him (Ex. 34:29–35). In this story and in the New Testament account of the Transfiguration (e.g., Matt. 17:1–9), a link is made between the Word of God and light, especially the light shining from a human countenance. The Word is a light, 'the true light that enlightens every man' (John 1:9), and the revelation of God incarnates itself as an image—a human being transfigured.

---

6 Aristotle, in *Poetics*, traces the arts back to a natural human instinct for 'imitation,' as well as for *harmony* and *rhythm*. It is tempting to see even in this division a rough echo of the Trinity (and thus of our trio of remembering, thinking, and speaking).

The dramatic arts (theater, opera) are arts of action, or the image in movement. They correspond to the Holy Spirit, as the medium of the unity of Father and Son, and as the 'gift' of one to the other.[7] This seems to capture the close partnership of image and movement that takes place in drama. Words are thrown into action as poetry. The 'new' element that arises from the synthesis of image and movement is the possibility of representing the adventure of the soul, a particular image of God caught up in a movement of exodus and return, of forgetting and remembering; at the same time partly responsible for and partly responsive to its fate.

In each case it is easy and natural to see how these elements can be woven into a school curriculum and its daily activity. Not everyone will be equally interested or gifted in a particular art, but the basic skills and interests on which the more refined expressions of art are built must surely be universal. The fine arts begin with lullabies and nursery rhymes, with hopscotch and running in the playground, with piling colored bricks into a heap and knocking it down, and with scratching rude images of teacher on the desk. But more importantly, these various arts accompany the arts of language and cannot safely be separated from them. For we are creatures of the imagination. Our very language is made up of images, which means that even the most seemingly abstract philosophy depends upon signs and metaphors. Our skill in remembering, thinking, and communicating depends to a large extent on our skill in manipulating images drawn from the senses, and thus on the range and mastery of our experience as bodily creatures.

History

But are we still not forgetting some important elements that would have to find a place in any real-world curriculum? I may well be accused of failing to integrate studies such as biology and history (more generally, the study of the natural world, and the

7 The Holy Spirit being described by Pope John Paul II, in his encyclical *Dominum et Vivificantem* (10), as 'Person-Gift'; as that which Father and Son give to each other in giving their whole selves unreservedly.

study of our own culture) that are of particular concern in the modern world.

Hugh of St Victor talks of 'history' in the later parts of his *Didascalicon* only in connection with the study of Sacred Scripture. We, I think, need to widen the focus. We could do so by noting, first, that the methods of study and the powers of mind that are developed through the Trivium do need to be applied to certain objects of study. Those objects can be considered to be three: the natural world, the world of culture, and the world of Scripture, each of which intrinsically possesses an historical dimension, since it unfolds or evolves through time. In fact Scripture, read with the eyes of faith, provides a key to the interpretation of the other two, and so has a certain primacy. But in each case, the search for truth leads us beyond the level of phenomenon and appearance to a deeper level of understanding; that is, beyond the visible world to the invisible principles of order. We are always searching for the Logos, whether we do so by examining the wings of a fruit fly or the origins of the Second World War.

Just as we saw in the case of the expressive or creative arts, a Catholic curriculum can draw on the profound wisdom of the liberal arts tradition, and the Trivium in particular, to integrate a whole range of potential studies. These studies, however, will no longer be considered mere 'specializations' fragmented one from another. They will be considered, rather, as interiorly related by the fact that all are aspects of or pointers to an underlying truth that unites them all, which the religious believer grasps as their common origin in God, the 'living Mind' and 'sole primordial Idea or Pattern of things' (Boethius).

To read Scripture solely according to the historical or literal sense, as some biblical scholars have done, is to miss the vital spirit and unity of the text. The literal sense is the support for a doctrinal, a moral, and a mystical sense, which together raise our minds and hearts to God, revealing Christ as the One in whom we live and move and have our being (Acts 17:28). But nature too—from the stars to the beetles, from the cells to the planets—needs to be read with an eye to what it reveals of God, his beauty and wisdom. In other words, the worlds of nature or human civilization when approached via the Trivium are encountered in a contemplative spirit, looking not just for facts but for meaning.

Let us apply this to history in particular. Although concerned primarily with higher education, Christopher Dawson's book *The Crisis of Western Education* is most helpful here. Dawson writes:

> The conversion and reorientation of modern culture involves a double process, on the psychological and intellectual levels. First, and above all, it is necessary for Western man to recover the use of his higher spiritual faculties—his powers of contemplation—which have become atrophied by centuries of neglect during which the mind and will Western man was concentrated on the conquest of power—political, economic and technological.[8]

Dawson argues for educational reform as the key to this recovery of the 'lost principle of integration' in our civilization. I would argue we need to reform 'from below' as well as 'from above,' and that the Trivium, no less than the Quadrivium, is the place for it. But I agree with Dawson that one of the components of the reform must be to introduce the study not just of history, which as such tends to fall into a heap of disconnected incidents ('one darn thing after another'), but of Christian culture, even (in an appropriate form) at the level of the younger student, whose imagination can only be kindled, after all, by a strong narrative. Ultimately Dawson sees the need for 'a study of the culture-process itself from its spiritual and theological roots, through its organic historical growth to its cultural fruits,' since it is 'this organic relation between theology, history and culture which provides the integrative principle in Catholic higher education, and the only one that is capable of taking the place of the old classical humanism which is disappearing or has already disappeared.'[9]

None of this is to say that other civilizations or views of history should not be taught or studied—indeed they should—but that in each case it is the inner unity or principle of coherence that is

---

8 Christopher Dawson, *The Crisis of Western Education*, 202.

being sought, whatever the field of study. There is no prospect of a child's education being constricted by such an approach, unless the underlying principles I have outlined have been completely misunderstood. 'Christian education should be wider, not narrower, than that of a secular school.'[10]

Dreaming a Catholic School

This book represents a quest for a vision of wholeness in education. I have tried to suggest ways in which that vision could be pursued at a theoretical level. But sooner or later one must try to put this vision into actual practice. What if one now had a free hand to start a Catholic 'primary school' (for, say, ages 5 to 11)? One would not necessarily want to follow any of the models and methods associated with the great educationalists. On the other hand, there is clearly a great deal to be learned from them. Let me suggest, in some detail—albeit very tentatively (inviting feedback and criticism from teachers and parents)—a few ideas that would be in line with the Christian child-centered philosophy I have tried to describe. Call this an exercise; I leave it to your imagination how to extend the experiment to the later age groups and into higher education. It may at least serve as a helpful transition to the next chapter, which is largely concerned with homeschooling, since much of what follows could be easily applied within the home, where the institutional restraints are much reduced.

9 Ibid., 137–8. He writes of classical studies and humanist culture that they formed the 'keystone' of the educational structure, and when it was removed from Catholic education 'the higher studies of theology and philosophy became separated from the world of specialist and vocational studies which inevitably absorb the greater part of the time and money and personnel of the modern university' (134). This separation is one manifestation of a more widespread phenomenon, which might be called the isolation and attrition of contemplation in favour of action, leading to the creation of a 'sub-religious' mentality 'sheltered from the direct impact of reality' and forced into social conformity (173).

10 Ibid., 187. For more of an outline of what Dawson means by the Christian 'culture-process,' see pp. 140–43; and, of course, his many historical works.

Dreaming a Catholic School

There may well be better ways of implementing a design based more explicitly on the three elements of the Trivium, and I have made suggestions here and there to that effect already. Here I want to make the point that the elements of the Trivium (even in the broader meaning I have given them) do not necessarily need to be used explicitly as the framework of the curriculum, since the philosophy behind them can inform any number of other models, especially when one has in mind the youngest children. In order to give an idea of what I mean, I propose to sketch a primary curriculum quite loosely around the following five elements, not three: (a) storytelling; (b) music; (c) exploration; (d) painting and drawing; (e) dance, drama, and sport.

In each of these interrelated areas, other important educational concerns can be addressed as follows. (1) Religious education would be incorporated in each section through the use of religious stories, art, and history, set within an appropriate doctrinal framework (in Catholic schools this would be provided by the Catechism of the Catholic Church, or for younger ages an appropriate simplified form of this). (2) Built into each section would be an education in the use and meaning of symbols, numbers, and geometric shapes (seeing forms, reading signs, making connections and comparisons). (3) In each subject area there would be opportunities to develop the fundamental skills we have been discussing throughout this book, such as thinking, remembering, and communicating (logic, rhetoric, grammar, memorization).

I mentioned that for Dorothy Sayers the Classical Curriculum is built on the assumption of three main developmental stages. It is assumed that a child will first acquire basic skills and vocabulary, then move on at a slightly later age to applying these skills in developing the ability to argue and analyze, and finally achieve proficiency and a degree of intellectual mastery—moving from concrete to analytical to abstract thinking. I suspect this is too programmatic, and that in reality the stages cannot be so easily distinguished (especially in the early ages). So in what follows I will leave open for discussion the question of how exactly the teaching will be adapted to the developmental stage of each child. First, here are some thoughts on each of the five main elements of the curriculum.

(a) STORYTELLING. Children live mainly in their imaginations, and are continually learning, making up, and acting out stories in the playground and elsewhere. But it is not just children; even grown-ups tell themselves stories (more often than not in their case it is the same story over and over again). We make sense of the world around us by turning our lives into a story where we are the hero (or victim). In fact every human life is a quest, which is why such stories are culturally universal. The school should recognize the importance of the imagination in learning, and make group storytelling (as if around a campfire or hearth) and reading aloud a feature of the curriculum. The education of the imagination is the education of the heart. Through the choice of stories the children can be introduced to history as well as traditional fairy tales, myths, and classic tales, as well as being encouraged to develop narrative skills of their own and to develop the confidence to speak in a group. Stories can be illustrated or acted out, creating links with the other areas of the curriculum. This is also the best way to draw children into the learning of language, and indeed languages.

(b) MUSIC. We have tended to compartmentalize (not to mention commercialize) music in our culture, but for the ancients it was a fundamental element in education. We also tend to assume that musical ability is a rare gift, whereas in fact nearly everyone responds to some aspect or type of music, and most can be taught to sing or to play an instrument. I once met a musician who had formed an orchestra out of street children in an abandoned village in Lithuania, awakening in them a sense of community and confidence in their own abilities. Again the theme of Music can be connected to Story or Exploration or Dance, and it can be taught historically or with reference to religion. Sounds and patterns of sounds can be analyzed into simple numbers and shapes, thus introducing the children to mathematics by the back door. By exploring the relationship between music and lyrics in popular songs, a range of literary skills can be developed.

(c) EXPLORATION. Children are natural explorers, curious about each other and about the world around them. Some, of course, are more adventurous than others, while some are naturally risk-averse. Nevertheless, this tendency can be harnessed for educational purposes. Whether the teacher decides to explore the local neighborhood or the geography of the wider world, outer space using actual telescopes or the images available from Hubble and NASA, different cultures using story and music, the world of the very small through microscopes and magnifying glasses, abstract patterns through the construction of simple geometric figures, or the worlds of the past, the direction lessons take will to some extent be shaped by the interests of the class. The study of nature through direct contact with gardens, animals, and wilderness is indispensable. A basic principle of this whole approach to education is that everything is connected to everything else, and so we should not be afraid of the particular interests or obsessions of the children—follow one interest, however narrow it appears, and it will open up one subject after another, making each in turn appear 'interesting' for the first time. (This is a lesson we can take from the unschooling or 'free school' movement—see next chapter.)

(d) PAINTING AND DRAWING. In every lesson in each of the five areas, there will be a time for sitting and listening, or watching a demonstration, but especially with young children attention spans are short and teaching is more effective if it involves them actually doing things. Arts and crafts provide an obvious opportunity to explore, express, and interiorize what is being learnt each day, to develop particular skills based on the coordination of hand and eye, and to refine the ability to observe the world around. The construction of simple geometrical shapes and the construction of mobiles and models also entails an exploration of spatial relationships and proportions. Drawing found objects, local scenery, or the faces of one's friends is another kind of exploration. A good teacher can use comic books and cartoons to develop an interest in art and stylization, as well as storytelling. Famous paintings in galleries and books, or religious icons and architecture, can be shown to be full of symbols as well as interesting patterns. Modern education tends not to pay attention to the symbolic properties of things, but symbols, metaphors, and analogies help to connect everything together. Here, as in the other classes, the teacher can often use the children's own interests and insights as a starting point.

(e) DANCE, DRAMA, AND SPORT. The kind of whole-body activity that goes on in the playground (although many games even there are of course quite formal) can be channeled into the more disciplined activity of role-playing and performance on the stage and in the gym. Here music and storytelling, as well as the arts and crafts, and social skills such as a capacity for teamwork, all have an important part to play. Some children will be naturally more suited to chess than football or acrobatics, but a measure of physical exercise and discipline is appropriate for everyone. We can also learn a great deal from the experience of other cultures with Tai-Chi or Yoga without fearing the corruption of our civilization by alien philosophies. The links between music, dance, sport, and acting are obvious. Dramatic productions developed in class are an opportunity to bring together the whole range of educational elements in a single activity involving teamwork.

Now, here are some comments on the three 'skill sets.'

(1) RELIGIOUS EDUCATION. Clearly religion needs its own space in the curriculum, but I am assuming that in the early years this may be in the form of liturgy, common prayer, or assembly rather than in a separate instructional class. (I assume religious instruction will also take place in the home and parish.) My suggestion is to integrate religion into the curriculum throughout. Religious stories, symbols, images, designs, and music will provide multiple opportunities to bring the children into contact with religious truth—the existence and providence of God, our own calling to happiness with him beyond any partial fulfilment in this world, the fact that God is love and died for us on the Cross, the reality of the presence of Christ and his Spirit in the Church and sacraments. That is not to say that every subject is to be turned into an opportunity for catechesis. The teacher is not a preacher. I am simply saying that we should not *exclude* religion from any other subject.

The inter-religious question is of course a tricky one, especially if the class contains children from different faiths. A Catholic teacher should have to make no apology for teaching elements of the Christian faith as true, provided three principles are remembered. First, much of what we believe is revealed by God and therefore cannot be proved by reason, which makes it understandable that some people do not share our beliefs. It is necessary to acknowledge that fact. Second, questions on any matter are always welcome and faith has nothing to fear from reason. Other religious traditions contain truth, goodness, and beauty as well—which is why they have given birth to civilizations. Just as we need not fear reason, we need not fear to recognize beauty in another person's belief. Third, our own faith teaches that we must respect the freedom of others. Everyone is loved and called by God, but everyone's journey is different and in the end they must be allowed to find their own way with God's help. What we believe is important, but just as important is how we act and behave towards each other.

(2) SEEING THE FORM. The keys to meaning are form, gestalt, beauty, interiority, relationship, radiance, and purpose. An education for meaning begins with the perception of form. Education should open our eyes to the meaning and beauty of the cosmos. In the search for beauty as well as truth, the arts and sciences can be reunited in the common enterprise of civilization. Thus, just as the curriculum presents a myriad opportunities to communicate religious truth and ethical values, so it presents opportunities to lead the children into the appreciation of form. That is why I have not suggested distinct classes on arithmetic or geometry (or art appreciation or music theory). The study of shapes and numbers (and the shapes numbers make, for example in simple mathematical processes, in 'magic squares,' puzzles, and multiplication tables) should take place naturally within other classes, where it can be seen to be integrated with everyday life and connected with everything under the sun—both in a practical sense and in terms of *theoria* or contemplation (beginning with the mere enjoyment of the beauty in harmony, symmetry, and ratio).

(3) BASIC SKILLS. Thinking, remembering, communicating, calculating: these are basic skills that need to be developed in every subject area. In modern progressive education they have been neglected, leading at times to an over-reaction in conservative schools where they may be drilled into children more assiduously. My suggestion is that these skills are best developed naturally in contexts where they can be seen to be of use in the

pursuit of particular interests. A child preparing to perform in a play will naturally need to learn a number of lines. One who is asked to explain a particular hobby to the rest of the class will need rhetorical skills. Stories and essays and poems require the learning of grammar and vocabulary. They can also be fun—for example, the use of medieval 'memory palace' techniques, or the invention of secret languages and codes.

VI

Learning in Love

Parents as Educators

The role of parents in education is of such importance that it is almost impossible to provide an adequate substitute. The right and duty of parents to educate their children are primordial and inalienable.[1]

THIS BOOK has touched on many themes—no doubt too many, though the case for inclusion of each was overwhelming. But it is time to bring the remaining threads together, and we may do so by returning to the fundamental relationship in education, and the fundamental unit of society, namely the family into which we are born or adopted. (Conscious of how many people have experienced a broken family, let us simply define 'family' as the place where we are loved. It may or may not be with the parents who gave birth to us.)

There is another theme that should be highlighted here. At the beginning of the book I did not want to emphasize the negative too much, but John Senior voices a pressing concern that many educators today share. Though a supporter of the Great Books approach, he has found that most students 'simply don't have the prerequisites such an education supposes.' They have not 'exercised and purified their imaginations' in the 'thousand good books that children and adolescents used to read before they tried the great ones.'

In my own direct experience teaching literature at universities, I have found a large plurality of students who find, say,

1 *Catechism of the Catholic Church*, para. 2221.

Treasure Island what they call 'hard reading,' which means too difficult to enjoy with anything approaching their delight in *Star Wars* or electronic games.[2]

He has found they read too slowly, and without the needed concentration. As a result, publishers have been putting out annotated and abridged editions of the children's classics (and, of course, for better or worse Disney fills in the gaps). Those who notice the problem and call it 'dumbing down' are very concerned about the shrinking of children's attention span. But there is a further problem. Senior noticed that the problem is not only with books, or language, but with things. It is 'experience itself' that has been missed:

> There is no amount of reading, remedial or advanced, no amount of study of any kind, that can substitute for the fact that we are a rooted species, rooted through our senses in the air, water, earth and fire of elemental experience. . . . When you plant even the best children's literature in even the brightest young minds, if the soil of those minds has not been richly manured by natural experience, you don't get the fecund fruit of literature which is imagination, but infertile fantasy.[3]

Those great books celebrate and explore and assume some contact with the world of direct everyday experience of 'fields, forests, streams, lakes, oceans, grass, and ground' of which most modern children have been deprived. More than 50% of the world's population now live in cities, for the first time in history. Even those who live outside an urban environment are increasingly raised within a virtual one. In England and America there has been much concern in recent years that the need to protect children from a range of dangers from automobiles to pedophiles

2 John Senior, *The Restoration of Christian Culture*, 186. Flannery O'Connor makes a similar point with characteristic pungency in *Mystery and Manners* (137): 'In other ages the attention of children was held by Homer and Virgil, among others, but, by the reverse evolutionary process, that is no longer possible; our children are too stupid now to enter the past imaginatively.'
3 Ibid., 188.

has prevented them playing outside in the relative freedom that was enjoyed by their parents and grandparents.

The effects of all this are hard to measure or predict, but they certainly distance students from the literature of the past. It may be that human artistry will flow into new channels, with images replacing words in a new 'iconological' environment just as rich as the old verbal one, but I suspect much will be lost along the way. We need to bear all this in mind in what follows. I have brought it up now because the home is the place where the foundations are laid, and homeschoolers—even if they send their children to school later (and these children form the backbone of the new liberal arts colleges in America)—are the ones who today are fostering the ability to read and think and experience in traditional ways. With well over two million children being home-educated in the US alone, this constitutes a considerable cultural force. The starting point is always reading (and playing music) to the child as soon and as much as possible.

Cultivating the Moral Imagination

There is a particular kind of experience that our society too often fails to provide, and it is found in stories that nurture and build the moral imagination. This is the theme of Vigen Guroian's book *Tending the Heart of Virtue*. Here the term 'moral imagination' refers, very loosely, to a way of looking at life—or, as Guroian puts it, the 'process by which the self makes metaphors out of images given by experience,' which it then employs 'to find and suppose moral correspondences in experience.'[4]

The key word here is *metaphor*, whose root meaning in Greek refers to a process of 'carrying over' or 'carrying beyond.' A metaphorical word or phrase carries us from something to something else by suggesting a likeness or analogy. All of poetry and most of language is based upon this power of suggestion. It is the key to the discovery of meaning, and to that 'intercommunication' that I touched on and presupposed in the chapter on Rhetoric, and

---

4 Vigen Guroian, *Tending the Heart of Virtue*, 24.

the reason for the importance I gave to Storytelling in the previous chapter. Guroian reports that his students are increasingly unable to 'recognize, make, or use metaphors.' They are perplexed by novels that require them to find 'inner connections of character, action, and narrative.'[5] They seem unable to read 'symbols,' because they have been trained only to search for 'facts,' which require little or no interpretation.

It is the imagination that interprets, that gives meaning to the world, by 'joining the dots,' discovering the otherwise invisible connections between things, events, and qualities. Its ancient Greek patron is Hermes, or Mercury, the messenger of the gods and inventor of fire. Thus to discover meaning is to connect, to travel from one thing to another, or to go on a journey. But to go on a hike without landmarks or direction, or on a sea voyage without sail, sextant, compass, or map, is the same as being lost, or wandering aimlessly, a victim to every wind that blows. In this particular metaphor, the journey is meant to correspond to our path through life in search of happiness—and this reduces, ultimately, to the search for meaning, for an adequate reason for living, which can only be given to a human life by love.

The basic human need to 'find our bearings' explains why, as Guroian states at the very outset of his book,

> Children are vitally concerned with distinguishing good from evil and truth from falsehood. This need to make moral distinctions is a gift, a grace, that human beings are given at the start of their lives. Of course, we mustn't mistake this grace for innocence.[6]

Our innate moral sense, revealed in childhood by the desire to divide the world into goodies and baddies, and to insist on fairness (even if only as a cover for getting what they want), has deep roots. We fail to nourish those roots at our peril—often, as Guroian points out, thanks to a deeply flawed notion of individual

5 Ibid., 25. And no doubt the same inability will make it hardly possible to relate to the language and gestures of the Catholic liturgy, which is built up entirely of metaphor, analogy, and symbol.
6 Ibid., 3.

autonomy that leads us to think we are respecting our children's freedom by encouraging them to determine for themselves (like Adam and Eve) what is right and what is wrong. *Values* are not the creations of the self, as Nietzsche suggested when he started using the term in its plural form. Moral limits and absolutes are not the bars of a cage but the walls and floors of the house of Being, the home of the human heart. Without them we would find ourselves back in the howling wilderness with nowhere to go.

Guroian's book examines in detail the powerful metaphors and moral principles embodied in some of the great stories, including *The Velveteen Rabbit* and *The Little Mermaid*, *The Wind in the Willows*, *The Snow Queen*, *Beauty and the Beast*, and the *Chronicles of Narnia*. Each is different, but each reveals an aspect of what it is to be truly human, not in a moralistic way by spelling out the rules and regulations of right behavior, but in a way that educates the imagination of the reader to see patterns linking characters, decisions, and events in the real world. It is a way not just of communicating the rules, but showing how the rules work and perhaps even why they work. However fantastic and unreal the landscapes in which these stories unfold, however untrue to life they may be in a factual sense, they are true in the deeper meaning of the word, in that they reflect the way things really are. They open our eyes to look not merely at the surface of things, but at their form.

With all this in mind, it makes sense to regard reading stories aloud to one's children the archetypal act of the Trivium. One is simultaneously remembering a tradition, revealing the Logos, and (by voice, inflection, and gesture) dramatizing a story to communicate that meaning 'heart to heart.'

Education of the Heart

Mother Frances Xavier Cabrini (1850–1917), foundress of the Missionaries of the Sacred Heart of Jesus in Italy, sent by Pope Leo XIII to found orphanages, schools, and hospitals in America, coined the phrase 'education of the heart' (the cultivation of a 'feeling for God in an environment of affective relationships in which education becomes an act of love') to describe her philosophy of education. The phrase 'education of the heart' has an immediate resonance, of course, but we can connect it more explicitly with the themes of this book by recalling the meaning of the 'heart' in Christian tradition as we did on pages 84–85.

The *Philokalia* sums up the ancient Biblical and Patristic tradition. The 'heart' for Biblical Christianity, say the English editors of this classic anthology of spiritual writings,

> is not simply the physical organ but the spiritual center of man's being, man as made in the image of God, his deepest and truest self, or the inner shrine, to be entered only through sacrifice or death, in which the mystery of the union between the divine and the human is consummated. 'I called with my whole heart,' says the Psalmist—that is, with body, soul, and spirit.[7]

The 'innermost aspect' of this heart they identify with the organ of contemplation, the intellect or *nous*, which knows the truth through direct experience or intuition, unlike the lower reason or *dianoia* which operates on the basis of abstract concepts and deductions. In Scholastic terms it is the *synderesis* or 'spark' of conscience, where the knowledge of good and evil are 'written on our hearts' (Jer. 31:33; Rom. 2:15). This is the inner chamber into which our Lord asks us to withdraw in order to pray, so that 'your Father who sees in secret will reward you' (Matt. 6:6). It is the inner precinct, the 'Holy of Holies' in the Garden of Eden where the Tree of Life springs up.

Mother Cabrini, with her devotion to the Sacred Heart, would have known all of this quite well. The Sacred Heart of Jesus is not simply the physical organ but the whole Person of Jesus gathered into one and given in love (just as when we talk about 'giving our heart' in romantic love we mean that the whole person is dedicated to and poured out for the other). The flourishing of the devotion after the eventual canonization of the seventeenth-century visionary Margaret Mary Alocoque corresponded to an awakening of metaphysical intuition and of affective mysticism in

---

7 G.E.H. Palmer, Philip Sherrard, Kallistos Ware (eds), *The Philokalia*, vol. 2, 383.

response to the rationalism and Jansenism of the time, but devotion to the radiant Heart is found everywhere in Christian mysticism. The Heart of Jesus pieced by the centurion's lance on the Cross is also, of course, identified from the earliest times as the source of the sacraments (represented by the blood and water that came from the wound), so that the death of Christ, voluntarily undergone as an act of love in order to save us, becomes the source of our eternal life.

The education of the human heart, then, represents not merely a training of the emotions, but an integration of feelings and thoughts into a higher unity: that of the conscience or intellect that is our point of contact with God in the deepest recesses of our soul. It is a bringing about of self-knowledge in the possession of virtue, as Plato described in the *Meno*.

Charlotte Mason

Born in Wales in 1842, Charlotte Mason was educated at home and then became a teacher. Some of her lectures to parents were published, inspiring an organization called the Parents' Educational Union (PEU) and its periodical. A devout Christian, she founded a training school at Ambleside in Cumbria, renamed Charlotte Mason College after her death in 1923.

Mason was nothing if not realistic. She is not writing for idealized middle- or upper-class families, and is well aware of the challenges involved. 'The parent who would educate his children, in any large sense of the word, must lay himself out for high thinking and lowly living; the highest thinking indeed possible to the human mind and the simplest, directest living.'[8]

Her 'Preface to the Home Education Series' in the same volume makes clear that already in 1896 her philosophy of education, which she put forward as tentative but which was based on long and varied experience, anticipates the principles I have been struggling to establish:

8 Charlotte Mason, *Parents and Children*, vol. 2 of Charlotte Mason's Original Homeschooling Series, 170. Series published online at *www.amblesideonline.org/CM*.

The central thought, or rather body of thought, upon which I found, is the somewhat obvious fact that the child is a person with all the possibilities and powers included in personality. Some of the members which develop from this nucleus have been exploited from time to time by educational thinkers, and exist vaguely in the general common sense, a notion here, another there. One thesis, which is, perhaps, new, that Education is the Science of Relations, appears to me to solve the question of curricula, as showing that the object of education is to put a child in living touch as much as may be of the life of Nature and of thought. Add to this one or two keys to self knowledge, and the educated youth goes forth with some idea of self management, with some pursuits, and many vital interests.

Mason's books are a feast of wisdom, in many ways as applicable today as when they were first written. Nothing I say should discourage you from reading them for yourself, which is easy enough to do online. The final and most realistic volume of her series, published in 1922 (forty years after her first), is called *Towards a Philosophy of Education*, and is probably the best place to start. In it she writes:

> Here is a complete chain of the educational philosophy I have endeavored to work out, which has, at least, the merit that it is successful in practice. Some few hints I have, as I have said, adopted and applied, but I hope I have succeeded in methodizing the whole and making education what it should be, a system of applied philosophy; I have, however, carefully abstained from the use of philosophical terms.

> This is, briefly, how it works:

> A child is a Person with the spiritual requirements and capabilities of a person.

> Knowledge 'nourishes' the mind as food nourishes the body.

> A child requires knowledge as much as he requires food.

> He is furnished with the desire for Knowledge, i.e., Curiosity; with the power to apprehend Knowledge, that is, atten-

tion; with powers of mind to deal with Knowledge without aid from without—such as imagination, reflection, judgment; with innate interest in all Knowledge that he needs as a human being; with power to retain and communicate such Knowledge; and to assimilate all that is necessary to him.

He requires that in most cases Knowledge be communicated to him in literary form; and reproduces such Knowledge touched by his own personality; thus his reproduction becomes original.

The natural provision for the appropriation and assimilation of Knowledge is adequate and no stimulus is required; but some moral control is necessary to secure the act of attention.

A child receives this in the certainty that he will be required to recount what he has read. Children have a right to the best we possess; therefore their lesson books should be, as far as possible, our best books.

They weary of talk, and questions bore them, so that they should be allowed to use their books for themselves; they will ask for such help as they wish for.

They require a great variety of knowledge—about religion, the humanities, science, art; therefore, they should have a wide curriculum, with a definite amount of reading set for each short period of study.

The teacher affords direction, sympathy in studies, a vivifying word here and there, help in the making of experiments, etc., as well as the usual teaching in languages, experimental science and mathematics.

Pursued under these conditions, 'Studies serve for delight,' and the consciousness of daily progress is exhilarating to both teacher and children.[9]

---

9 Charlotte Mason, *Towards a Philosophy of Education*, vol. 6 of Charlotte Mason's Original Homeschooling Series, 18–19. Series published online at *www.amblesideonline.org/CM*.

She also writes in the same place that 'We should allow no separation to grow up between the intellectual and "spiritual" life of children; but should teach them that the divine Spirit has constant access to their spirits, and is their continual helper in all the interests, duties and joys of life.' Secularized versions of Mason's ideas and methods exist, but the depth of her approach is evidenced in her refusal to strip grace away from nature. Such remarks are more than window-dressing, more than moralism or fideism. She really has a sense that children possess a spiritual life and that this is the most important dimension of their being— the source of their freedom and happiness.

This is not the place for a detailed review of homeschooling curricula, but there are plenty of books, periodicals, publishers, websites, and blogs that offer guidance to parents wanting to take this route.[10] But before you make a decision, you might want to consider an even more radical alternative.

John Holt

John Holt brought to a head many of the child-centered theories we discussed earlier. In his view, all children are naturally curious, but they develop at different rates and have very different interests. This curiosity should be the engine of education; but to force them all into a one-size-fits-all curriculum damages them and does untold damage to society. In fact he regarded the 'school'—a place which is purpose-built to separate learning from everyday life—as a pernicious invention, the foundation of the modern 'slave state.' The answer is to 'de-school' (in the phrase of Ivan Illich, another major influence in this area after his book *Deschooling Society* appeared in 1971), to take children out of schools, and not merely replicate the structures of the school within the home but do something entirely different. The phrase that came to be used of Holt's movement was 'unschooling.' It

10 A good introduction might be *The Catholic Homeschool Companion*, edited by Maureen Wittmann and Rachel Mackson. Catholic spiritual guidance for homeschoolers can be found in Chantal R. Howard, *The School of the Family*.

meant that children would learn whatever they needed in life—including the vital ability to learn new things—entirely by pursuing their own interests. They would be shaped by their own families (Holt saw the family as the fundamental unit of society) and by their own choices, rather than by the state or by the ideological preferences of the school board.

Born in 1923 and raised in New England, Holt was a teacher who became disillusioned with schools and published his first book, *How Children Fail*, in 1964. In it, he argued that the main cause of failure was fear, and that fear was endemic in schools. A more positive theory, *How Children Learn*, followed in 1967. Children are natural learners, he thought, and the best context for learning is everyday life. He set up a home education newsletter and a mail-order book-service, and through his books and lectures became a major influence on the philosophy of education until his death in 1985.

One advocate of unschooling expresses it like this:

> While few of us get out of bed in the morning in the mood for a 'learning experience,' I hope that all of us get up feeling in the mood for life. Children always do so—unless they are ill or life has been made overly stressful or confusing for them. Sometimes the problem for the parent is that it can be difficult to determine if anything important is actually going on. It is a little like watching a garden grow. No matter how closely we examine the garden, it is difficult to verify that anything is happening at that particular moment. But as the season progresses, we can see that much has happened, quietly and naturally. Children pursue life, and in doing so, pursue knowledge. They need adults to trust in the inevitability of this very natural process, and to offer what assistance they can.[11]

The best introduction to unschooling for Catholics may be a book edited by Suzie Andres called *A Little Way of Homeschooling*, based on the experiences of a group of homeschooling families

---

11 Earl Stevens, 'What Is Unschooling?' at *www.naturalchild.org/guest/earl_stevens.html*, accessed 27 May 2011.

who saw in John Holt the articulation not just of a theory but of a spirituality of education, akin to the Little Way of St Thérèse of Lisieux—a way of trust and simplicity. Though John Holt had no religious affiliation, and no one claims he was a saint, the method he recommended bore a striking resemblance to that of the most recent Doctor of the Church. Being based on the actual experiences of families over many years, the book builds a certain confidence that unschooling is not merely an ideology, and need not be considered an impractical, idealistic dream.

There is in fact a deep compatibility between the radical homeschooling or unschooling approach to education and other manifestations of the Catholic understanding of human nature. Natural Family Planning, like unschooling, is regarded by many as an impractical ideal or an ideology, but when practised in the right spirit it reveals itself as something else entirely. The point about NFP is that it requires mutual respect and attentiveness to the whole person of the spouse. It should not be treated as just another instrument for achieving the aim of reducing fertility. For a couple to master NFP is for them to grow in mutual love and knowledge. Similarly, unschooling is based on respect for the child and love between generations.

And yet the accounts in the book underline one important fact. It seems that, to be realistic, one must acknowledge that the success or failure of the unschooling as well as the homeschooling approach depends in large part not just on the individual child and his motivation, but on the family as a whole, especially the parents. We have already seen how vital the relationships within the family are, and how the flourishing of any individual requires the right kind of attention from others. Precisely because unschooling is a spirituality, it will only succeed (on almost any measure of success) if the family is of a certain type or has a certain maturity. As Cindy Kelly says in her chapter, 'The most powerful way to encourage my sons to enjoy a new area of learning is to model it myself and continue our dialogue about their interests and mine.'[12] Not every parent is capable of that; not all have the leisure, confidence, or motivation to do so.

12 Suzie Andres, *A Little Way of Homeschooling*, 35.

Formal schooling is not just a cage where children can be kept while the parents earn the money to buy food and to pay the mortgage and taxes. Sometimes it can offer children a few hours of freedom in each day where they can escape the enormous pressures of a dysfunctional family.

The Holy Family

These days we are uncomfortably aware that many, sometimes most, families are broken or damaged, and that far from enjoying support, children may need to find a refuge from their parents. 'Normal' or 'happy' families are becoming increasingly uncommon. It is impossible to calculate the cost—spiritual and psychological as well as merely economic, generation after generation—of the damage inflicted on children by their families when love is absent or replaced by malice. Yet it is a source of hope, even in such situations, that since (as the saying goes) love is stronger than death, it is certainly stronger than hate. If the wounds inflicted by evil cannot be entirely healed, they can—like the wounds on Christ's body, which still appeared after the Resurrection—be glorified, becoming a source of something positive.

In Christ's case, those wounds were not just evidence that he was the same person who had suffered and died, nor mere trophies reminding us of his victory, but—according to a widespread mystical tradition—a place for sinners to take refuge. That is, the signs of vulnerability in his physical body remain places of vulnerability in a spiritual sense, where he may be approached and entered into. A wound, if you think about it, is an occasion when what is within us is exposed, when the life-blood is poured out and becomes accessible to others. In Christ's case, what is within him is love, the Holy Spirit. The places where human sins inflicted pain on him are the very places where, because that pain was accepted on our behalf and for our sake, Christ's love was most fully expressed. The wounds are the ways he reaches out to us, invites us into his body, shares his blood with us.

Something similar applies to psychological wounds, which

of course cut much deeper than physical ones. Christ had no psychological weakness to be played upon, no inner vulnerability as most of us do. Nevertheless, in the same way that he accepted the punishment for sins he did not commit, or the pain that comes from having sinned even though he never did, we may suppose that he was willing to suffer the consequences of having been betrayed and abused as a child, though he never was, since this too is a consequence of human sin. When on the Cross he was abused and scorned, when he felt abandoned by his Father, or deserted or betrayed by his friends, he chose to experience these things in solidarity with those who as children had lived through horrors we quail to imagine as adults. He used his own experiences of suffering to create a sacramental connection between their suffering and his.

The Cross is a gateway, a threshold, a bridge, a ford. Through the Eucharist and other sacraments we are brought to that place which Mary and the disciple John occupied at the foot of the Cross, when the Church was born, and we enter through the Cross into a new family, the Holy Family—if we are willing, which is to say, if we receive the Spirit that is being offered.

In this way every member of the Church can say that he has 'left father and mother' for Christ's sake, and become part of a new family, like John the beloved disciple who 'took Mary into his home.' He has become a child again, in order to enter the kingdom of God. His life is now being homeschooled, and his home is with Mary. That is, whether or not we remain closely involved with our natural families, those previous relationships with father, mother, sisters, and brothers are dissolved as we enter a new state of existence.

We are in the place where we can learn to be whatever God wants us to be.

Conclusion

Beauty in the Word

IN THIS book I have been concerned with students or pupils who are children, and what the liberal arts tradition (creatively interpreted) might have to say about their education. This tradition aspires to educate us in freedom and responsibility. I have tried to sketch some of the philosophical and theological foundations of this tradition of education, and hinted how this might be expressed within schools and homes, wherever children are educated.

Now begins the serious task of working with parents and teachers to develop applications of the ideas in this book not only for primary schools but for the older children, from eleven to eighteen, as part of a wider project involving many other people. In the Endnotes will be found some detailed discussions that would have distracted us from what was already a complex set of arguments if they had been placed in the main text.

But as this book comes to a close, I hope that it is clear why the title *Beauty in the Word* seemed so appropriate for this stage of our project. Why do we desire truth? What makes the Word of God attractive to us? Immediately these questions take us into the realm of (Platonic) *eros* and of beauty. We desire the truth because it is beautiful, it draws us towards it. In fact, to be drawn towards something, to desire it, is part of what we mean by calling it 'beautiful.'

Here is the paradox. We may be drawn to truth by beauty, but truth is beautiful to us because it is true. The beauty of anything really lies in its truth. I don't mean, of course, that every truth we discover must be beautiful in the superficial sense of being pretty. There are plenty of ugly truths. In the film *The Matrix*, on revealing the ugly truth of mankind's true state to Neo, Morpheus uses the phrase: 'Welcome to the desert of the real.' And yet Neo would rather know the truth, however ugly, than be kept in a state of illusion.[1] Not everyone is as brave as Neo, even within the film, but on some level we surely all know that the 'real' has so many levels of meaning and richness, and that it is interconnected with everything else in such complex and elegant ways, that it cannot help being more beautiful *as truth* than any lie or delusion, even if we cannot hope to see that beauty at first.

To become conscious of truth, goodness, and beauty—the three transcendental qualities of Being, whose ultimate home is in the Word—seems to have a lot to do with being human. As far as we can tell, the other animals are lost in the task of being themselves. They do not agonize about who they are or speculate about why they might be here. Nor do they stand apart from the other creatures in order to give them names, as we do (as Adam does in Genesis and we have been trying to do ever since). Our self-consciousness is part of what gives us our unique capacity for freedom. Man is a speaking animal, a self-reflexive animal, an animal with a certain liberty, and therefore a 'metaphysical' animal. To know, to love, to rejoice in another, to rejoice in that which is not the self, is the privilege of one who stands apart, and who is capable of making the distinction between self and other.[2]

In any relationship of knowledge, love, and joy there is always an intimation of that which transcends us. The experience of the 'transcendental properties of being' constitutes the dawn of metaphysics, and it takes place in us at a very early age. According to Hans Urs von Balthasar, it happens at the moment when we first recognize our mother's smile. He writes:

> The infant is brought to consciousness of himself only by love, by the smile of his mother. In that encounter, the horizon of all unlimited being opens itself for him, revealing four things to him: (1) that he is one in love with the mother, even in being other than his mother, therefore all being is

---

1 Another classic movie that carries the same message is Peter Weir's *The Truman Show.*

2 Thus it was that Etienne Gilson said that man may be defined as a creature 'who knows other beings as true, who loves them as good, and who enjoys them as beautiful' (*The Unity of Philosophical Experience*, 255).

one; (2) that that love is good, therefore all Being is good; (3) that that love is true, therefore all Being is true; and (4) that that love evokes joy, therefore all Being is beautiful.[3]

Our humanity is bound up with our capacity to realize that Being (and therefore everything that exists, in one degree or another) is one, good, true, and beautiful. When we are brutalized into ignorance of this fact, or denied the experience of it, the taste of it, then we have become less than human.

It should be pretty obvious how this relates to what I have been saying about education. The fact that *Being is an expression of love* is the foundation for humane education. A rediscovery of Being, of metaphysics—of the kind Pope John Paul II called for in *Fides et Ratio*, in which faith and reason go hand in hand— implies a rediscovery of love. The 'civilization of love' that we hope and long for would be one in which the metaphysical dimension of all things has been recovered. We could then also speak of a recovery of the sense of the sacred. John Paul II writes:

> Wherever men and women discover a call to the absolute and transcendent, the metaphysical dimension of reality opens up before them: in truth, in beauty, in moral values, in other persons, in being itself, in God. We face a great challenge at the end of this millennium to move from *phenomenon* to *foundation*, a step as necessary as it is urgent. We cannot stop short at experience alone; even if experience does reveal the human being's interiority and spirituality, speculative thinking must penetrate to the spiritual core and the ground from which it rises.[4]

---

3 H.U. von Balthasar, *My Work in Retrospect*, 114. See also D.C. Schindler, *Hans Urs von Balthasar and the Dramatic Structure of Truth*. Schindler points out (117) that what is revealed in the primordial awakening to love is also a fifth point: the child's worthiness of being loved, or the goodness of the child's own being. It is this alone that can awaken the child's whole being in response. I should add that Balthasar does not explicitly address what happens if the mother never smiles—or is never present. Presumably Being must then find some other way to reveal itself as one, true, good, and beautiful. For more on the relationship of Beauty and Wisdom see Endnote 8.

4 John Paul II, *Fides et Ratio*, n. 83.

Moving 'from *phenomenon* to *foundation*,' from creatures to their common Being, we see all things as full of light. They are radiant because they are created, and therefore they are essentially intelligible, knowable, communicable. Their essence, i.e., what they are in themselves, is thought by God, and therefore thinkable by us. As the great Thomist Josef Pieper reminds us, 'The measure of the reality of a thing is the measure of its light'—in fact 'the reality of things is itself their light.'[5] And this also implies interconnection, for light is that by which we see other things. It is in the light of each thing that we see all others, and this is the root of the unity of knowledge, the intrinsic connection between every subject, every interest, with every other (provided you look hard enough!). All are connected through the Logos, the Word, which is the light of the world, refracted through a million creatures.

In the vision of Denys the Areopagite, and the Christian Platonism adapted and integrated by St Thomas, which is the tradition within which I want to situate a Catholic philosophy of education, the entire cosmos is a cascade of light pouring down from the Father of Lights. He is at the same time intimately present as Creator with each thing in its own degree, intending and loving and sustaining it in existence. That light is the divine communication of meaning, existence, and form, descending and ascending through the Son of Man who is the radiant center on which all converge. He, the Word, is also the Light Incarnate, the source of the world's beauty and wisdom.[6]

5 Josef Pieper, *The Silence of St Thomas: Three Essays*, 56. For a larger collection of essays on several themes related to the present book, see Josef Pieper, *For the Love of Wisdom*.

6 'Christ is the Transcendent One who, creatively emanating, immanentizes Himself in His creatures. He is, thus, the radiant center of each. Denys reads His Presence in all. In the midst of all creatures abides the incandescent Christ' (William Riordan, *Divine Light*, 151).

Coda

Blessed John Paul II

'YOU WILL learn the truth and the truth will make you free' (John 8:32). Jesus' words, given to us in John's Gospel, are a decisive reference point for outlining *some perspectives on the mystery of education*. In the verse just cited, Jesus juxtaposes the two components—truth and freedom—which man frequently finds difficult to coordinate properly. Indeed it can be remarked that, while in the past a form of truth far removed from freedom sometimes prevailed, today we often witness the exercise of freedom far removed from truth.

A person however is free, Jesus states, only when he recognizes the truth about himself. This naturally involves a slow, patient and loving process by which one can gradually discover one's own being, one's own authentic image.

It is precisely in this process that we find the figure of the educator as the person who, by helping in ways like those of a father and mother to recognize the truth about oneself, cooperates in the achievement of freedom, 'an exceptional sign of the image of God' (*Gaudium et Spes*, 17). In this perspective, the teacher's task, on the one hand, is to testify that the truth about oneself is not limited to a projection of one's own ideas and images, and on the other, to introduce the student to the marvellous and ever surprising discovery of the truth that precedes him and over which he has no control.

But the truth about ourselves is closely linked to *love for ourselves*. Only those who love us possess and preserve the mystery of our true image, even when it has slipped from our hands.

Only those who love can educate, because only those who love can speak the truth which is love. God is the true teacher because 'God is love.'

Here again is the core, the incandescent center of all educational activity: co-operating in the discovery of the true image which God's love has impressed indelibly upon every person and which is preserved in the mystery of his own love. Educating means recognizing in every person and speaking about every person the truth that is Jesus, so that every person may be set free. Free from the slavery forced upon him, free from the slavery, even more rigorous and terrible, which he imposes on himself.

The mystery of education is thus closely linked to the mystery of *vocation*, that is, the mystery of that 'name' by which the Father called and predestined us in Christ even before the world's foundation.[1]

1 John Paul II, 'The Teacher's Task is to Witness to the Truth,' address to the plenary assembly of the Congregation for Catholic Education, 14 November 1995. Translated in *L'Osservatore Romano*, English weekly edition, 29 November 1995.

Endnotes

1. *The Seven Liberal Arts* (pp. 9, 61, 92, 105)

The liberal arts tradition, as Christopher Dawson writes in *The Crisis of Western Education*, is

> practically as old as the Confucian tradition in China and has played a similar part in forming the mind and maintaining the continuity of our civilization.
>
> [It] had its origins some twenty-four centuries ago in ancient Athens and was handed down intact from the Greek sophists to the Latin rhetoricians and grammarians and from these to the monks and clerks of the Middle Ages. These in turn handed it on to the humanists and school-masters of the Renaissance from whom it finally passed to the schools and universities of modern Europe and America.[1]

Unlike the educational systems of the Oriental cultures, 'it was not confined to a priestly caste, or the study of a sacred tradition, but formed an integral part of the life of the community,' since it developed 'in the free atmosphere of the Greek city state, and its aim was to train men to be good citizens; to take their full share in the life and government of their city.'[2]

With Plato and his Academy, the 'liberal arts' (not yet definitively seven in number) were deemed preparatory to the study of philosophy and the contemplation of ultimate truth.[3] This emphasis was largely lost in the western Roman Empire, where the worldly disciplines of rhetoric / oratory and law became more

---

1 Christopher Dawson, *The Crisis of Western Education*, 6.

2 Ibid.

3 See *Republic* Book 7, especially 527d–e concerning the 'useless subjects' by which the eye of the soul is purified and rekindled, 'more important to preserve than ten thousand eyes, since only with it can the truth be seen.'

prominent (Cicero, Quintilian). With the advent of Christianity, merging the Classical traditions of Greek philosophy and Roman law with the study of biblical and theological writings, the liberal arts were again subordinate to Theology.

During the period of barbarian invasions and conversions in the West, a synthesis of Classical and Christian learning was preserved mainly in the monasteries, until at the end of the eighth century with Charlemagne and the ninth with King Alfred in England a wider revival of learning and a vernacular culture could begin to develop (in Alfred's case, Dawson points out, with a greater emphasis on history and natural theology than on grammar and rhetoric).

Writing in the fifth century, St Augustine already assumes that the liberal arts number seven in all (whereas the Classical writer Varro had spoken of nine). Indeed he tells us he had been in the process of writing books on the seven liberal arts at the time of his conversion.[4] The number seven is underlined by Augustine's pagan contemporary Martianus Capella in a heavily allegorical account of the *Marriage of Philology and Mercury*, in which Philology is the earth-born daughter of Wisdom, Mercury the inventor of letters—mortal and immortal respectively—and the seven arts their bridesmaids, with Music included in the seven rather than Medicine or Architecture because she is more concerned with heavenly matters. With Boethius (d. 525) the word *Quadrivium* first becomes established as the name for the four mathematical sciences; with his contemporary Cassiodorus the seven arts are identified with the biblical 'seven pillars' of Wisdom; and a century later Isidore, Bishop of Seville, incorporates them definitively into his encyclopedic *Etymologies*.

Thus by the time of the twelfth-century Renaissance, and the creation of those self-governing guilds of students and teachers we know as universities (beginning with the law school of Bologna and the medical school of Salerno), the seven liberal arts are already well established by ancient tradition. Naturally they are

4 In *De Ordine* (AD 386). Augustine's *On Christian Doctrine*, concerned mainly with how to read Scripture, does not explicitly address the seven arts, but exerted an enormous influence on the later development of the tradition.

expanded, if not exploded, in later centuries by the influx of new or recovered learning from the ancient world, transmitted by the Arabs or Byzantium—making possible the fifteenth-century Renaissance and the ensuing transformations of European civilization.

The present book is concerned mainly with the foundational Trivium or language arts, beginning with Grammar, the first art taught by Mercury/Hermes (from whom we get the word hermeneutics, meaning 'interpretation'). The Quadrivium, on the other hand, is concerned with mathematical symbols—that is, with numbers and shapes, together with their relations. The four arts of the Quadrivium begin with two, Arithmetic and Geometry, on which the other two are based. Arithmetic is the study of the properties and behavior of numbers (as the Circe Institute puts it, 'What happens to seven if it meets five? What will eight do if we multiply it by four?'), while Geometry concerns the behavior of shapes and patterns. Arithmetic requires us to pursue order through time, since numbers accumulate successively when we perform the operation of counting. Music involves appreciation of these temporal patterns and the relationships between them. It depends on our ability to perceive a mathematical form that is spread out through time (the time it takes for a symphony or a song to unfold). Geometry involves the perception of forms that are spread through space as well as time, hence its foundational relationship to Astronomy, which concerns the geometrical relationships of the heavenly bodies—the world of 'light.' Music is the study of ratios and proportions, and Astronomy of shapes in motion. (See my *Beauty for Truth's Sake*.)

2. Conscience (pp. 28, 51)

In his little book *Conscience*, Romano Guardini gathered together a series of addresses on 'self-education' to young people in Germany in the 1920s, in an 'age that has been laid waste,' an age of the 'degradation of the spirit.' He was writing in a Germany that would soon elect Hitler as Chancellor, but his comment applies also to our own time of rampant consumerism. He first establishes the reality of the Good and of conscience as our 'organ' for perceiving it (*Conscience*, 17). The good is that which is, at any given moment, appropriate, fitting, and right in relation to the objective situation. Conscience is the ability to recognize what is good and translate it into action. But conscience does not come fixed and ready-made; it has to grow and develop as we open ourselves to life and allow ourselves to be taught. How does this happen? Guardini speaks of the practice of 'recollection' as the awakening and living of one's unique soul as the only way to give life its meaning and purpose. This recollection 'around a spiritual center' involves the clearing and expansion of an inner space or depth through the discipline of the senses and the attention. We are always allowing ourselves to be torn between what is no longer, and what is not yet; we must try to 'create a present' for ourselves, which means 'pulling ourselves together' from a state of distraction and scattering by means of solitude, silence, and prayer; not just eliminating what is useless and resisting temptation, but turning our attention towards that which is within and beyond the self, the living spiritual center or inward light that is our point of contact with God.

Pope Benedict (writing before his election as pope) identifies the deepest, ontological foundation of the phenomenon we call 'conscience'—the law 'written on their hearts' of Rom. 2:15—as 'something like an original memory of the good and true (the two are identical),' and therefore as an *anamnesis* of the Creator.'[5] This is also, he says, the foundation of mission or evangelization, because the Word that the believer brings to another is not fundamentally alien to him, but involves an awakening to his own existence as constitutively related to God, a kindling of his own *anamnesis* of the Origin. Without that assurance it would lose its justification.[6]

Ratzinger is looking back not just to Plato and St Paul but to the Scholastic distinction between *conscientia* and *synderesis*. The latter is used most commonly in this tradition to refer to the fundamental knowledge of moral norms or principles or the inclina-

---

5 'Conscience and Truth,' 535.

6 In the terms of this book, Rhetoric (*Ethos*) in a sense depends on Grammar (*Mythos*), or Remembering.

tion towards these, whereas 'conscience' refers to the application of these norms to particular cases. Thus *synderesis* is the 'spark' or *scintilla* of conscience (Ratzinger calls it 'the spark of love')—the very summit of the mind. This is the highest point of the soul, which according to St Jerome, in a commentary on the four-faced cherubim in Ezekiel, is the 'spirit' in man not extinguished by the Fall, but which, like an Eagle flying above the other three faces—the Man, the Lion and the Bull—rises above the rational, the irascible, and the appetitive parts of the soul. It is the 'gravity' of the soul towards goodness and away from evil, the deepest mark of the divine image, our point of communication with God. Consequently for St Bonaventure this is the faculty that contemplates God not as Being, but as the Good, and not as One but as Three (as Bonaventure puts it, 'the *most blessed Trinity* in its name which is the Good').[7]

3. *Information Revolutions* (p. 50)

In his book *The Dignity of Difference*, Britain's Chief Rabbi, Jonathan Sacks, describes the development of the computer and the internet as the most recent of four great 'information revolutions,' each of which has transformed human consciousness and civilization. The first was the invention of writing. Writing began with pictographic signs or symbols inscribed or incised on bricks, and quickly became a way of representing speech in linear mode. 'For the first time knowledge could be accumulated and handed on to future generations in a way that exceeded, in quantity and quality, the scope of unaided memory' (129).

But the early forms of writing were complex and could only be mastered by a small elite group prepared to invest the time in learning a vast number of symbols. The second revolution opened writing to everyone by the invention of the alphabet. 'For

7 I am citing here my own essay in Cunningham and Candler (eds), *The Grandeur of Reason*, and St Bonaventure from the *Itinerarium Mentis in Deum*, where *synderesis* is the 'sixth wing' of the Seraph who represents the human faculties on the way to God. On the 'Spark of Divine Love' see also Barry R. Pearlman, *A Certain Faith*, 193–7.

the first time the entire universe of communicable knowledge was reduced to a symbol-set of between 20 and 30 letters, small enough to be mastered, at least in principle, by everyone' (131). The alphabet was invented, Sacks says, by the Semitic peoples of the Middle East, in the age of the biblical patriarchs. It made possible a society of universal literacy and equal dignity—the people of the 'book,' a book that enshrined a covenant between God and man freely entered into on both sides. 'Here, even more than in the city-states of ancient Greece, is born the idea of a free society' (134).

The third revolution is then the invention of printing, by which the book itself is made universally available—beginning with Luther's tracts and the Bible itself, millions of copies of which were in circulation by 1700.

The list might be extended by adding the drawing of pictures, which preceded the invention of writing, and the development of numbers, which followed it. But the pattern is already clear. Technology takes a human ability such as speech or memory and exteriorizes it, enabling its power and effects to be multiplied. Thus writing gave birth to civilization. What will the internet bring?

4. *Logos* (p. 60)

In Greek the word *logos* had a variety of uses. It meant, among other things, speech, account, reason, definition, rational faculty, and proportion. It is not essential to follow the evolution of the term, but the story may be of interest to some readers.

For the pre-Socratic philosopher Heraclitus, *logos* is the name of the underlying organizational principle of the universe, related to its common meaning as proportion and therefore harmony, but also identified with a material element—the cosmic fire. Plato used the word rather more abstractly, meaning an analytical account, distinguishing it from *mythos* or a fanciful tale of the gods. In the *Republic* 534b he refers to the dialectician as someone who can give an account (*logos*) of the true being of something— this being the goal of the process of division (*diairesis*) described in the *Sophist*. Plato's student Aristotle later uses *logos* as a synonym for the 'definition' of a whole, or else to mean reason or rationality, particularly in an ethical context. He also understands *logos* as mathematical proportion or ratio (from which we get the word 'rationality').

The Roman Stoics employed the word in a way reminiscent of Heraclitus to refer to the divine principle of organization, the fiery, active seed-force in the universe. As such it is the foundation of their theory about cosmic sympathy and natural law (*nomos*). But they distinguished an interior *logos* (equivalent to what we call thought) from an exterior *logos* (equivalent to speech). It was the Jewish Platonist writer Philo of Alexandria (d. AD 50) who identified the Logos with the divine Reason containing all the *eide* or 'ideas' that inwardly shape creation according to the Mind of God. As *kosmos noetos* the Logos could be described as a 'noetic' or intelligible cosmos preceding the visible one, or as even the divine Word or 'elder Son of God.' In the visible world (*kosmos aisthetos*), the Logos is the archetypal 'bond of the universe' holding all things together, reminding Christians inescapably of Col. 1:17 and the teachings of the Fourth Gospel.

John the Evangelist—for whom the Logos is the divine nature of the Son of God—is a contemporary of Philo, and since there is apparently no direct influence from one to the other, one may see this similarity either as an example of convergence (perhaps under a common Platonic-Pythagorean influence), or as a demonstration of the fact that the Christian teaching was already implicit within the texts of the Jewish Scriptures, waiting to be unpacked.

5. A Philosophy of Being (pp. 76, 86, 88)

It is, of course, not sufficient to criticize Descartes on the grounds that he broke with medieval philosophy, or that his own philosophy was so unconvincing. The search for clear and distinct ideas is a noble philosophical task. We need to see more clearly where he actually went wrong. This was the aim of Edmund Husserl, the founder of phenomenology, who at the dawn of the twentieth century went back to Descartes and tried to establish a new and more secure foundation for philosophy and scientific thought by attending to 'the things themselves' as they reveal themselves in consciousness.[8]

Husserl was followed by others, including Heidegger, who broke with him on various grounds. One of the most interesting splinter-groups was that of Adolf Reinach, who sought to develop his initial insights in a more 'realist' direction. These disciples of Husserl could see the power and the importance of the phenomenological method of attending to 'things in themselves,' but they were unhappy with 'bracketing,' as Husserl did, the question of mind-independent existence, thus effectively dissolving the self. In their hands, phenomenology recovered a doctrine of objective knowledge. Overcoming Descartes, it found itself back at the feet of Plato.[9]

The scene was set for a dialogue not only with the Greeks but with their Christian heirs, Augustine, Aquinas, and Bonaventure—a reintegration of modern philosophy with the Catholic tradition. We find this taking place, for example, in the book *Finite and Eternal Being* by Husserl's onetime assistant (and later Carmelite martyr) Edith Stein, and also in the work of Karol Wojtyla, the Polish philosophy professor who became John Paul II, especially in his major work *The Acting Person*. According to Wojtyla, the self is not in fact identifiable with the inner ground

8 Husserl took from Brentano (who in turn had borrowed it from Catholic scholasticism) the notion of consciousness as 'intentional,' meaning that it is always directed in some way to an object. Awareness is always 'of' or 'about' something; it is not completely blank. Husserl's early disciples believed that in this way classical objectivism or realism had been vindicated. After 1905, however, Husserl argued that in order to examine experience one must suspend any judgment about existence. Phenomenology became purely a doctrine of essences, of being as revealed in consciousness. Although this method of 'bracketing' or *epoché* was akin to Descartes' systematic doubt, it seemed to be a way of overcoming Cartesian dualism, for now the question of the objective existence of matter simply dropped out of view. It made no sense to speak of anything other than experience. Like some Asian mystic, Husserl was teaching that a Transcendental Ego is the ground of everything, prior to the polarity of self and other, subject and object.

9 This school of thought culminates in the work of the scholars associated with the International Academy of Philosophy and especially in Josef Seifert's book *Back to Things in Themselves*.

of consciousness discovered by phenomenology. The 'I' in 'I am' is revealed less through introspection than through action — the action not of a mind, but of a whole person.[10]

Wojtyla's analysis of human consciousness thus centers around its 'reflexive' function — the awareness of oneself as the subject of one's own acts and experiences; in other words, the revelation of oneself not as object or as idea, but as actor in the world.[11] Descartes thought we could know ourselves before we know anyone else, but in fact we can only discover ourselves in others or through others, by turning outwards and discovering ourselves in relationship.[12] It is in the eyes of the other that I find my true identity, just as it is perhaps the mother's smile that first awakens me to self-awareness as an infant.[13]

This discovery of the acting self, of the 'I am,' presupposes memory in a way that Descartes' and Husserl's discoveries do not, because the freely acting self is free only to the extent it is self-possessed, recollected, and receptive of its own nature, across the time of its existence.

10 'Since Descartes,' Wojtyla writes, 'knowledge about man and his world has been identified with the cognitive function. . . . And yet, in reality, does man reveal himself in thinking or, rather, in the actual enacting of his existence...?' And he adds, 'In fact, it is by reversing the post-Cartesian attitude toward man that we undertake our study: by approaching him through action' (Karol Wojtyla, *The Acting Person*, vii–viii). One of the best studies of Wojtyla's thought is Kenneth L. Schmitz's *At The Center of the Human Drama*. Schmitz puts it this way: 'A realist by intent, Wojtyla has appropriated tools used mostly by idealists in order to introduce subjectivity into realism' (74). In a parallel development, the philosopher Maurice Blondel had concentrated his attention on human action and subjectivity in his 1893 thesis *L'Action* at the Sorbonne. The text and Blondel's subsequent work was controversial but helped lay the foundations for the modern Catholic *ressourcement*. See Oliva Blanchette, *Maurice Blondel*.

11 Kenneth L. Schmitz, *At the Center of the Human Drama*, 73–7.

12 Cf. Marjorie Grene, *The Knower and the Known*, 86.

13 We find in Hans Urs von Balthasar an understanding of the foundations of human awareness that complements Wojtyla's. At the beginning of *Theo-Logic* I, without explicit reference to the philosophers and movements whose mistakes he is trying to avoid, Balthasar conducts his own phenomenological

Being, not the self, is prior to the distinction between object and subject, and the reason why Descartes and his successors were left needing to prove the existence of an external world, whereas the medievals (and other 'sane men') were not, is that he started on the purely subjective side of the divide. He reduced being to thinking. But the act of being which makes something what it is does not depend simply on me. And this in turn implies that to know a thing as given in reality involves not just the intellect but the will and the memory; not just an automatic awareness of it, or an intuition, but a yielding and a giving to it, a bringing close and a standing-back-from, which transforms both subject and object in something like the way a marriage transforms the couple.

This is much closer to our everyday, commonsense view of reality—the one we have before all the philosophers come along to confuse us. I exist in a world of objective things that differ from myself, and any knowledge of them is based on a relationship established through my senses. All this philosophical work—the refutation of relativism and idealism—lies behind John Paul II's statement in his first encyclical, *Redemptor Hominis* (1978), that 'Man remains a being that is incomprehensible to himself, his life is senseless, if love is not revealed to him, if he does not encounter love' (RH, 10).

The self is necessarily invisible to itself and can be discovered only in a relationship with the other, through love. The encounter with love, and the response to that encounter, is the drama of the human person though which he may be said to 'enact' his existence. It is in this way that he discovers his own nature, not as a consciousness, a mind, or a ghost in a machine, but as a full-blooded person. He discovers at the same time Being, which

---

meditation on the concept of truth that emphasizes the reciprocal relationship of subject and object in the act of consciousness. The subject discovers being (including its own) by receiving the object and serving it: 'only in going out of itself, in creatively serving the world, does the subject become aware of its purpose and, therefore, of its essence.' (H. U. von Balthasar, *Theo-Logic*, I, 62). And the object can be revealed only in the space provided by the subject, in which it becomes more than it was. For a comparison of Balthasar's phenomenology to that of Husserl, see the rich article by D.C. Schindler, 'Metaphysics Within the Limits of Phenomenology,' listed in the Bibliography.

reveals itself as pure gift and therefore as love made concrete in the other, in the self, and in the relationship between them.

6. *Laws of Thought* (p. 81)

Grammar, Logic (Dialectic), and Rhetoric are closely interconnected though distinct. The standard modern textbook is *The Trivium* by Sister Miriam Joseph CSC, who was inspired by the work of Mortimer J. Adler of the University of Chicago. Here I want to focus on the nature of Logic in particular.

In the text I refer to the Principle of Identity and Difference, the Principle of Contradiction, and the Principle of the Excluded Middle. These are the three classic laws of thought attributed to Aristotle and appropriated by the Scholastic tradition. The law of Identity simply states that a thing is always the same as itself ('A is A'). The law of Contradiction states that two contradictory statements cannot both be true at the same time and in the same respect ('A is B' and 'A is not B'). The law of Excluded Middle states that any proposition (statement of fact) is either true or not true ('either A is B, or A is not B'). These laws seem obvious enough, although of course they have been much discussed during the long history of philosophy.[14] The intention in formulating them is to derive certain basic notions of consistency and coherence that apply to all human thought about reality.

When we move beyond pointing and naming into the realm of making statements about things, we use our vocabulary and the rules of Grammar to do so. But it is necessary to test the truth of

---

14 It is possible that the Principle of Identity needs to be refined in the light of Christian revelation. If every being is constitutively related as gift both to God (its creator) and to other beings, there is no such thing as a simple identity of something with itself alone. In fact, without at least *three terms* we cannot define the identity of any *one thing*, either with itself or with another. Let's call this the 'Principle of Dynamic Identity,' after Pavel Florensky who first defined it. It is most obvious in the case of personal relations, where every 'I' implies a 'Thou,' every 'Thou' implies a 'We,' and every 'We' implies an 'I' and a 'Thou.' With this conception of dynamic identity we can overcome the modern dualism between subject and object. There is no 'subject' in the universe that is without an 'object,' or cut off from community. All subjectivity is relational.

any statement by examining it in two ways: are we being consistent or coherent in what we say, and does what we say correspond to what is the case? What we know—which provides the premise or starting point of our argument—comes to us through our own senses or (by our faith in another's testimony) through the senses of another, or else it is grasped intuitively in some other way. General propositions (like the three laws themselves) are based on an inductive judgment of this kind. The key to moving from fundamental agreed premises to an undeniable conclusion is maintaining, at each stage of the deduction or inference, both internal consistency (abiding by the three laws) and a correspondence to the real world.

The scientific method is particularly helpful, being based on careful observation under controlled conditions, in maintaining that link with reality, but it also requires logical thought to be applied to the observations, in order to separate what is essential to the thing's nature from what is accidental. And of course not all statements are empirical or scientific—poetic, moral, and historical statements can all be either true or false, although the application of the laws of thought will vary depending on the type of statement being made.

At this point a grammarian might add that, just as important as the aforementioned laws of thought in understanding the way language works is the principle of analogy, which is the way we connect one thing with another that is neither exactly the same (univocal, identical) nor completely different (equivocal, dissimilar), but shares certain characteristics with it. Analogies enable us

---

See Pavel Florensky, *The Pillar and Ground of the Truth*, esp. 344-8, and cf. Robert Slesinski, *Pavel Florensky*, 109–114. In my interpretation of the Principle, the identity of A is not simply A, but implies another (B) in relationship to it; and not just one other but at least two (B + C), to prevent a collapse of the dualism once again into monism. Thus A = A (+ B + C); B = B (+ A + C); and finally C = C (+A + B). Applied to the Trinity, 'Father' implies 'Son' + 'Spirit,' 'Son' implies 'Father' + 'Spirit,' and 'Spirit' implies 'Father' + 'Son'—or as Florensky puts it, 'Truth contemplates Itself through Itself in Itself' (ibid., 113). This does not allow us to *deduce* the Trinitarian relations from our observations of the world, but it does trace the relationships intrinsic to creatures back to their source in God.

to draw together and compare things that are different in kind yet somehow similar; to explore an obscure or newly discovered area in terms of what is already known and familiar; to make metaphors, illuminating one thing by comparison with another; to represent what is beyond our direct or ordinary experience, principally the inner and spiritual world, God, etc.; and to span large areas of experience, even the whole universe, in a single synoptic idea, such as being, action, power, goodness, knowledge, life, love, etc.[15]

Dialectic needs Grammar, and Logic needs Analogy, which is at the foundation of poetry, theology, and science. Things are never unrelated or completely unlike other things—the world is analogous through and through. 'The fundamental criterion, which gives us the authority to speak analogically, is that the unity which being possesses rests ultimately upon the unity of God, who is Being in act.'[16] Thus theologians talk of the 'analogy of being' enabling us to know something of God through analogy with his creation.[17] The analogy of being is equivalent to the idea of levels of reality. All beings resemble Being, both individually and in their relations to each other, by which they form a hierarchy of wholes.

7. Ethical Theories (p. 91)

A full survey of all the varieties of moral theory may be found in books by Pinckaers and others referred to, but it may help

15 W. Norris Clarke SJ, *The One and the Many*, 45.

16 Barry R. Pearlman, *A Certain Faith*, 35. Pearlman's book effectively demonstrates the use of analogy in apologetics and theology.

17 Hans Urs von Balthasar explores the interplay between dialectic and analogy in the Protestant theologian Karl Barth. In his early dialectical phase, Barth regarded the difference between God and creation as so great that the use of a common term like 'being' (however qualified) must be ruled out. In later writings he admitted an analogy between God and creation, but only on the basis of God's revelation in Christ (the analogy of faith rather than the analogy of being, or rather the latter *inside* the former, thus subordinating philosophy to theology). See Balthasar, *The Theology of Karl Barth*, 64–167, and the important discussion of nature and grace in Catholic theology (especially 267–325).

to think of these theories as divided into two main branches, as follows:

1. The Natural Law tradition	2. The Voluntarist tradition
Aquinas, etc. (Realists)	Ockham, etc. (Nominalists)
Emphasis on virtues	Emphasis on commandments
(as powers of the soul)	(what is to be done or not done)
What it is good *to be*	What it is good *to do*
Freedom *for*	Freedom *from*

The second tradition leads in the modern period to a split between 'deontological' ethics (ethics of duty, as in Immanuel Kant's philosophy) and 'teleological' or consequentialist ethics (ethics of goal, as in Jeremy Bentham and J. S. Mill), which supposes that we choose either on the basis of obligations and rules that determine what is right and wrong, or on the basis of what will bring about the greatest happiness of the greatest number.

Each of these modern positions and their various offshoots (including the ethics of authenticity developed in reaction to them by Nietzsche, the Existentialists, and analytic philosophers such as Bernard Williams) represent attempts to recover the balance that was lost when the Voluntarists abandoned the transcendentals, concluding that good and evil can have no ontological foundation other than (for theists) the will of God, and (for atheists) the will of man.

In other words, for the more balanced Natural Law tradition, some action was good or evil not merely because someone (e.g., God) had arbitrarily decided to call it that—and might just as well have done called it the opposite—but because it was good or evil in itself, and was willed or condemned by God because God is the all-highest Goodness to which that action corresponds (or not). God's omnipotence does not extend to the possibility of willing evil and good to change places, for omnipotence does not permit self-contradiction.

Servais Pinckaers terms the first kind of freedom (understood according to the Natural Law tradition) 'freedom for excellence,' and the other (in the Voluntarist tradition) 'freedom of indifference.' He illustrates the former as follows. There is a certain freedom in being able to bash at random on a piano, but a higher freedom that comes from submitting to the discipline that yields the ability to play music—similarly with the discipline that enables us to use language meaningfully and be understood by others; and something similar applies in the moral realm to the virtues. Growth in this higher kind of freedom, freedom for excellence, spirals closer and closer to something resembling the freedom of God himself, which is the perfect willing and doing of the good.

This has enormous implications for education:

> The length and complexity of moral education stem from the fact that freedom for excellence calls for the collaboration of all the human faculties and requires the patent work of coordinating them, which is achieved through exercise and experience. This work also requires acceptance of the help of educators and a dynamic openness to contributions and exchanges encountered in society, in a spirit of justice and friendship.[18]

And as he also says, 'It will not be a matter of choosing between a liberal or an authoritarian education, but of harmonizing freedom and authority in education and discerning the stages and seasons when it is best to emphasize authority or to favor initiative.'[19]

8. Wisdom: Mother of the Liberal Arts (pp. 8, 105, 135)

The liberal arts, beginning with the Trivium, have a 'Mother,' and that Mother is Wisdom, Sophia or Sapientia. We see Wisdom portrayed as a maternal figure in the allegorical art of the medieval cathedrals. But what is the relation of Wisdom to Beauty, and to the Word or Logos who is the center of universal meaning?

According to Aquinas's rather bland definition, beauty is 'that which, when seen, pleases.' (The word 'seen' has to be extended

18 Servais Pinckaers OP, *The Sources of Christian Ethics*, 373.
19 Ibid., 372.

to cover hearing and the other senses.) Thus it is for him the quality of pleasingness in things. Traditionally, though not necessarily by Aquinas, beauty is often included among the transcendental properties of being; in other words, it is defined as a property in some degree of everything that exists, the other 'transcendentals' being unity, truth, and goodness. So let me first try to define these transcendentals and then work out their relation to each other.

Unity refers to being as it is, because everything possesses first an identity with itself. So unity is the property which pertains to the being of something as it is in itself—the property of being itself and not another. The quest for *meaning* is essentially related to this unity, because the meaning of anything necessarily lies in its relation to the whole, or that to which it belongs and in which it participates. In other words, the unity of a thing does not isolate it, but gives it an interior relation to everything else. To the degree that something is a part of something bigger or more complex than itself, its meaning points to that greater whole, and so to the unifying principle that gives that whole its identity. A green leaf, taken by itself, only makes sense if we understand its relation to the tree, and to the sun, the nature of light and the process of photosynthesis, the molecules of which it is composed and where they come from, and the role it plays in the ecosystem. (Similarly, theologians can only make sense of evil and suffering by locating it within a universal plan or the story of salvation, so that its causes become clear along with the part it might play in the healing of the world's order.)

Truth is being as known. It is concordance with reality, with what is. Perfect truth is perfect concordance, amounting to identity. In this way truth and unity converge. The idea that truth is a property of things and not just of statements (or, to put it another way, that reality is a language in which things are statements or 'words') is important. In a sense, everything that exists is a 'word.' An effect reveals the nature of its cause, and so utters a truth about its cause. It is an 'expression' of its cause. In fact, it is the expression of the supreme Word, the Logos, which corresponds to being as a whole. You could say it is an echo of that Word, or an answer to it. We are 'called into being' by the Word, and addressed by Being. As creatures possessed of a degree of freedom, our behavior will help to determine the extent to which we conform to reality.[20]

Goodness is being as willed, or as loved. To be good is to be desirable, lovable, adorable, admirable. This implicitly refers to the dimension of freedom, of self-determination, just mentioned. Being is good because it is sought, it is the end in which things are fulfilled or completed. It is a resolution of tension, an overcoming of separation. Freedom is the movement of giving, by which the self determines its destiny, and by which it becomes more than it was before, ultimately becoming identified with the transcendent. God, of course, is perfect goodness because supremely desirable. In God freedom is the same as necessity, because there is no difference between his act of existing and his nature; but in all else, in everything created, there is a tension and a movement between what is and what might be or should be. This is the tension that is the source of all drama, all morality, all sanctity.

These three transcendentals correspond with the three phases or elements of the Trivium: Grammar, Logic, and Rhetoric. For as we have seen, at the most profound level these involve an awakening to unity in being, known as truth, and communicated in goodness.

What, then, of beauty? Beauty pertains to the liberal arts as a whole, and in its highest form may even be identified with the glory of God and with that Wisdom which is the 'Mother' of the seven arts of freedom.[21]

Beauty is coherence, harmony, proportion, fulfilment, perfect integration. In comparison with the others, I would say that beauty is being as enjoyed, as rejoiced in. This is what Aquinas was getting at with his notion of 'pleasingness.' When we confront a beautiful scene or object we feel a kind of joy. This joy, I

20 Cf. D.C. Schindler, *Hans Urs von Balthasar and the Dramatic Structure of Truth*, where this is developed, e.g. 230–37, 251–4, and chapter 5.

21 To anticipate slightly, I might quote Hans Urs von Balthasar from *The Glory of the Lord*, vol. 7: 'Theology: The New Covenant,' 524: 'The wisdom of God, which as such is oriented towards glory, is a wisdom that comes from the "depth" of God's personal freedom, and requires a free revelation through God's Spirit who is within him, just as much as a human "Thou" can disclose what is within himself only in freedom.'

think, always involves a feeling of liberation. 'For the experiences which should be produced by that which is really beautiful are wonder, and sweet amazement, and desire, and a pleasant fluttering of the wings of the soul,' Plotinus writes.[22] Our experience of beauty liberates or expands us beyond the boundaries of the self. The encounter with it arouses the desire to unite ourselves with it in order to become 'more' than we are.[23] At the same time, it may strike us as 'more than we deserve' or more than we have a right to expect.

Thus the joy associated with beauty is our pointer to the depths of Being in God. Interestingly, in the writings of both C. S. Lewis and J. R. R. Tolkien, the word 'joy' is associated with the obscure and poignant memory of this original depth-experience, this sense of a transcendent home. Lewis writes that once one experiences that joy, in German *sehnsucht*, one will always want it again.

> Apart from that, and considered only in its quality, it might almost equally well be called a particular kind of unhappiness or grief. But it is a kind we want. I doubt whether anyone who has tasted it would ever, if both were in his power, exchange it for all the pleasures in the world. But then Joy is never in our power and pleasure often is.[24]

This joy, 'poignant as grief,' is evoked by Tolkien in the cry of the seagulls and the music of the waves on the shores of Middle-earth, heard by the Elves who carry the memory of the distant West, and by the 'joyous turn' or eucatastrophe in fairy-tales, where a glimpse of paradise is attained after long temptation to despair.

22 Or in MacKenna's translation, 'wonderment and a delicious trouble, longing and love and a trembling that is all delight' (*The Enneads*, 1:6:4).

23 At the level of *eros* we recognize that there are two main ways to expand the self by uniting it with a desired beauty. The feminine way is to try to receive the beautiful into ourselves. The masculine way is to try to project or inject the self into the beautiful. At the spiritual level we do both of these things, and the Christian knows that both ways are rooted in God, who both receives himself and gives himself in the three Persons.

24 *Surprised by Joy*, 20.

As I hinted, beauty is sometimes excluded from the list of transcendentals, and there are several reasons for that, quite apart from the fact that it can easily be subsumed under goodness. One is the fact that the experience of beauty has a strong element of subjectivity, as if it were an attribute of ourselves rather than of being. I think it can be both. And what of the relation of being to God? If being and God were one and the same, any transcendental property would be rightly described as a property of God. This leads to the temptation to identify each of the transcendentals with one of the three Persons of the Trinity. Goodness or unity is associated with the Father, truth or beauty variously with the Son or Spirit, while unity or else beauty may also be associated with the Trinity as a whole. In that game of musical chairs, however, beauty is often left standing.

It seems to me, rather, that unity, truth, goodness, and beauty each analogously describes the divine nature as a whole, which is found complete and entire and undivided in each of the Persons. We might say, for example, that the self-giving of the Father to the Son and the Son's reception of the divine nature from the Father in the Holy Spirit illuminate the self-identity of each created thing (and therefore its unity), as well as its expressiveness (and therefore its truth), its perfection (and therefore its goodness), and its transcendence (therefore its beauty). Our experience of beauty, then, echoes the infinity of God—the fact that his own being is inexhaustible and therefore he is a continual delight to himself, a source of eternal rejoicing. The joy associated with beauty is our pointer to the depths of being in God. Meister Eckhart once said that 'God enjoys himself, and wants us to join him.'[25]

To say the Trinity reveals all these things is to say that Love reveals them, because Love is another name for the Trinity.[26]

---

25 Cited by J. Norris Clarke, *The One and the Many*, 238.

26 'Love is thus more comprehensive than being itself; it is the "transcendental" *par excellence* that comprehends the reality of being, of truth, of goodness,' as Gustav Siewerth puts it. Cited by Hans Urs von Balthasar in *Theo-Logic*, vol. 2: The Truth of God, 176–7. The citation occurs in a section of Balthasar's text where he discusses the relationship of the transcendentals to the Trinity.

Balthasar's seven-volume work, *The Glory of the Lord*, argues that creaturely being, or the common being of things around us in the world, which never exists by itself but only in dependence upon God and actually *in* individual things, once it is seen as transparent to the glory of God that is shining through it, mediates between God and ourselves. That is why we need to awaken our spiritual senses, to open our spiritual eyes to see this glory, this spiritual beauty. Without the metaphysical sense that enables us to look beyond the surface, things would be merely themselves, individual, opaque and disconnected, related one to another in an almost mechanical fashion. With it, things are transparent to something behind them, they are related interiorly to each other and to their source. Balthasar refers to *'creaturely reality in so far as it is seen and conceived as the all-embracing manifestation of God.'* [27] He even calls this, in a notable phrase, the 'kingdom of beauty.'

So here we have another clue to the relationship between beauty and being. Beauty is that which we see in things when we see them in the light of faith, plunged deep in the mystery of their own origin, sensing their dependence on an eternal Act we cannot see except in them. Beauty reveals something to us, something that draws us towards it, causing us to rejoice in anticipation.

This beauty exists in all things. We only need to open our spiritual eyes to perceive and receive it as such, and if we do it will lead us to God. The name Balthasar gives to the beauty that belongs specifically to God is 'Glory.' This is beauty in its fullness. Worldly beauty is the radiance of God's glory, shining through created being. It is 'cosmic *order* understood as *gift*.' [28]

The connection between Beauty, or Glory, and Wisdom is this. Wisdom is the 'idea' of creation, the manifestation and embodiment of the Logos, the goal to which the creation tends, and God's objective or purpose in creation. In that sense it both pre-exists the act of creation, and does not yet exist, and yet is

27 H.U. von Balthasar, *The Glory of the Lord*, vol. 4, 374.
28 David L. Schindler, *Ordering Love*, 348.

mysteriously present throughout from beginning to end. It is not the Logos, but is a 'bride' who can be seen first in the Virgin Mary, then in Ecclesia (the Church), and finally in the world united with God.

Wisdom is therefore the glory which was the Son's at the side of the Father before the creation of the world, a glory the Father bestows on him through his crucifixion in historical time, a glory which the glorified Son will then impart to the faithful when he gives them the Spirit, the Spirit of filiation, the Spirit of the Father and of the Son. Or rather, Wisdom tends through its whole being, in God as in ourselves, toward that divine glory which God gives to no other, but which is nevertheless destined to clothe all things, since all things, as we have said before, derive from the Father through the Son only to return to him in the Spirit.[29]

As mysteriously present here and now, and yet not fully manifest, Wisdom is the inspiration and goal of the liberal arts, which are like the pillars of the house she is building for herself in us. ('Wisdom has built her house; she has hewn out her seven pillars,' according to Prov. 9:1.) The memory of being, the pursuit of truth, the eloquence of the heart, and the musical mathematics of the cosmos and the soul, are the essence of the seven liberal arts. The beauty of Wisdom in all these inspires rejoicing, because it speaks of an ineffable reality on which everything depends, namely the love which is beyond Being because it rests in itself, in eternal delight.[30]

In that love is the source of all spiritual beauty, all glory, all Wisdom. It is beauty that moves us to love the one, the true, and

29 Louis Bouyer, *Cosmos*, 192. Cf. 'For wisdom is more moving than any motion: she passeth and goeth through all things by reason of her pureness. For she is the breath of the power of God, and a pure influence flowing from the glory of the Almighty: therefore can no defiled thing fall into her. For she is the brightness of the everlasting light, the unspotted mirror of the power of God, and the image of his goodness' (Wisdom 7:24–6, KJV).

30 We read in the Book of Proverbs that Wisdom is especially associated with *rejoicing* (and therefore with beauty): 'I was daily his delight, rejoicing before him always, rejoicing in his inhabited world and delighting in the sons of men' (Prov. 8:22, 29–31).

the good, not for her sake but for theirs. Perfect beauty is the form of love, the Trinitarian form of God—one in three, three in one—revealed to us through the life, death, and resurrection of Christ, and manifested in the creation built upon the seven pillars of Wisdom.

Bibliography

Lionel Adey, *C. S. Lewis' 'Great War' with Owen Barfield* (rp Rosely, Cumbria: Ink Books, 2002)

Carl Anderson and José Granados, *Called to Love: Approaching John Paul II's Theology of the Body* (NY: Doubleday, 2009)

Suzie Andres, *A Little Way of Homeschooling: Thirteen Families Discover Catholic Unschooling* (Lake Ariel: Hillside Education, 2011)

Aristotle, *Aristotle's Metaphysics*, trans. Joe Sachs (Santa Fe: Green Lion Press, 1999)

Augustine, Saint, *On Christian Doctrine* (NY: Macmillan, 1958)

————. *The Trinity*, trans. Edmund Hill OP, 'The Works of Saint Augustine,' part 1, vol. 5 (NY: New City Press, 1991)

Hans Urs von Balthasar, *The Glory of the Lord*, vol. 4: 'The Realm of Metaphysics in Antiquity' (San Francisco: Ignatius Press, 1989)

————. *The Glory of the Lord*, vol. 5: 'The Realm of Metaphysics in the Modern Age' (San Francisco: Ignatius Press, 1991)

————. *The Glory of the Lord*, vol. 7: 'Theology: The New Covenant' (San Francisco: Ignatius Press, 1989)

————. *My Work in Retrospect* (San Francisco: Ignatius Press, 1993)

————. *Razing the Bastions* (San Francisco: Ignatius Press, 1993)

————. *Theo-Logic*, vol. 1: 'The Truth of the World' (San Francisco: Ignatius Press, 2000)

————. *Theo-Logic*, vol. 2: 'The Truth of God' (San Francisco: Ignatius Press, 2004)

————. *The Theology of Karl Barth: Exposition and Interpretation* (San Francisco: Ignatius Press, 1992)

————. *Unless You Become Like This Child* (San Francisco: Ignatius Press, 1991)

Owen Barfield, *Romanticism Comes of Age* (Wesleyan University Press, 1966)

Benedict XVI, *Caritas in Veritate* (Vatican City: 2009). Papal encyclicals are available online at www.vatican.va. See also under Joseph Ratzinger below.

Oliva Blanchette, *Maurice Blondel: A Philosophical Life* (Grand Rapids: Eerdmans, 2010)

Bonaventure, Saint, *Itinerarium Mentis in Deum*, Works of Saint Bonaventure, vol. 2 (Franciscan Institute, Saint Bonaventure University, 1956)

Henri Bortoft, *The Wholeness of Nature: Goethe's Way of Science* (Edinburgh: Floris Books, 1996)

Louis Bouyer, *Cosmos: The World and the Glory of God* (Petersham: St Bede's Publications, 1988)

Stratford Caldecott, *Beauty for Truth's Sake* (Grand Rapids: Brazos, 2009)

———. *The Fruits of the Spirit* (London: CTS, 2010)

———. *The Power of the Ring: The Spiritual Vision Behind* The Lord of the Rings (New York: Crossroad Publishing Company, 2005; revised edn forthcoming 2012)

———. and Thomas Honegger (eds), *Tolkien's* The Lord of the Rings: *Sources of Inspiration* (Zurich: Walking Tree Publishers, 2008)

Carlo Caffara, *Living in Christ: Fundamental Principles of Catholic Moral Teaching* (San Francisco: Ignatius Press, 1986)

Nicholas Carr, *The Shallows: What the Internet is Doing to Our Brains* (New York: Norton, 2010)

Ernst Cassirer, *Language and Myth* (New York: Dover, 1946)

G. K. Chesterton, *The Common Man* (London: Sheed & Ward, 1950)

———. *The Defendant* (London: Dent, 1901)

———. *Orthodoxy* (New York: Dodd, Mead & Co., 1908)

———. *What's Wrong With the World* (Dodd, Mead & Co., 1910)

W. Norris Clarke SJ, *The One and the Many: A Contemporary Thomistic Metaphysics* (South Bend: University of Notre Dame Press, 2001)

Congregation for Catholic Education, *The Religious Dimension of Education in a Catholic School: Guidelines for Reflection and Renewal* (Vatican City: 1988)

Ananda Coomaraswamy, 'Nirukta = Hermeneia,' in *The Eye of the Heart* 1 (2008), 3–10. See www.latrobe.edu.au/eyeoftheheart.

Vincent Cronin, *The Wise Man from the West* (London: Rupert Hart-Davis, 1955)

Conor Cunningham and Peter M. Candler (eds), *The Grandeur of Reason: Religion, Tradition and Universalism* (London: SCM, 2010)

Christopher Dawson, *Progress and Religion: An Historical Enquiry* (London: Sheed & Ward, 1931)

———. *The Crisis of Western Education* (Steubenville: Franciscan University Press, 1989)

John Dewey, *Schools of Tomorrow* (NY: E. P. Dutton and Co., 1915)

Louis Dupré, *Passage to Modernity: An Essay in the Hermeneutics of Nature and Culture* (New Haven and London: Yale Univ. Press, 1993)

Pavel Florensky, *The Pillar and Ground of the Truth: An Essay in Orthodox Theodicy in Twelve Letters*, trans. Boris Jakim (Princeton University Press, 1997)

Etienne Gilson, *From Aristotle to Darwin and Back Again: A Journey in Final Causality, Species, and Evolution* (South Bend: University of Notre Dame Press, 1984)

———. *The Unity of Philosophical Experience* (San Francisco: Ignatius Press, 1999)

Marjorie Grene, *The Knower and the Known* (Lanham: University Press of America, 1974)

Bibliography

Luigi Giussani, *The Risk of Education: Discovering our Ultimate Destiny* (NY: Crossroad, 2001)

Romano Guardini, *Conscience* (London: Sheed & Ward, 1932)

_____. *The End of the Modern World* (Wilmington: ISI Books, 1998)

Malcolm Guite, *Faith, Hope, and Poetry: Theology and the Poetic Imagination* (Ashgate, 2010)

Vigen Guroian, *Tending the Heart of Virtue: How Classic Stories Awaken a Child's Moral Imagination* (Oxford University Press, 1998)

Chantal R. Howard, *The School of the Family: A Renaissance of Catholic Formation* (Phoenix: Leonine Publishers, 2010)

David V. Hicks, *Norms and Nobility: A Treatise on Education* (University Press of America, 1999)

Hugh of Saint Victor, *The Didascalicon of Hugh of Saint Victor: A Medieval Guide to the Arts*, trans. Jerome Taylor (New York: Columbia University Press, 1961)

Valentina Izmirlieva, *All the Names of the Lord: Lies, Mysticism and Magic* (University of Chicago Press, 2008)

David Jelinek and Li-Ling Sun, 'Does Waldorf Offer a Viable Form of Science Education?' (College of Education at California State University, 2003, online at www.postwaldorftutoring.com/html/ScienceWaldorfStudy.pdf).

John Paul II, *Fides et Ratio* (Vatican City: 1998). Papal encyclicals are available online at www.vatican.va.

John of Salisbury, *The Metalogicon: A Twelfth-Century Defense of the Verbal and Logical Arts of the Trivium*, trans. Daniel D. McGarry (Philadelphia: Paul Dry Books, 2009)

Sister Miriam Joseph CSC, *The Trivium: The Liberal Arts of Logic, Grammar, and Rhetoric* (Philadelphia: Paul Dry Books, 2002)

D.F. Krell (ed.), *Martin Heidegger: Basic Writings*, trans. Frank A. Capuzzi with J. Glen Gray (New York: Harper & Row, 1977)

Keith Lemna, 'Mythopoetic Thinking and the Truth of Christianity,' *Communio* (Spring 2010)

C.S. Lewis, *Of this and Other Worlds* (London: Collins Fount, 1982)

Arthur O. Lovejoy, *The Revolt Against Dualism: An Inquiry Concerning the Existence of Ideas* (London and New Brunswick: Transaction Publishers, 1996)

Marshall McLuhan, *The Classical Trivium: The Place of Thomas Nashe in the Learning of His Time* (Corte Medera: Gingko Press, 2006)

Jacques Maritain, *Creative Intuition in Art and Poetry*, The A.W. Mellon Lectures (London: Harvill Press, 1954)

Charlotte Mason, 'Charlotte Mason's Original Homeschooling Series,' published online at www.amblesideonline.org/CM. vol. 1, *Home Education*; vol. 2, *Parents and Children*; vol. 3, *School Education*; vol. 4, *Ourselves*; vol. 5, *Formation of Character*; vol. 6, *Towards a Philosophy of Education*

Livio Melina, *The Epiphany of Love: Toward a Theological Understanding of Christian Action* (Grand Rapids: Eerdmans, 2010)

Thomas J. Norris, *Getting Real About Education* (Blackrock: Columba Press, 2006)

Flannery O'Connor, *Mystery and Manners: Occasional Prose, Selected and Edited by Sally and Robert Fitzgerald* (NY: Farrar, Straus & Giroux, 1969)

Christopher Oleson, 'Rortian Irony and the Humility of Right Reason,' *Logos* 15:1 (Winter 2012), 13–49

G. E. H. Palmer, Philip Sherrard, Kallistos Ware (eds), *The Philokalia: The Complete Text compiled by St Nikodimos of the Holy Mountain and St Makarios of Corinth*, vol. 2 (London: Faber & Faber, 1981)

Barry R. Pearlman, *A Certain Faith: Analogy of Being and the Affirmation of Belief* (Lanham: University Press of America, 2012)

Josef Pieper, *For the Love of Wisdom: Essays on the Nature of Philosophy* (San Francisco: Ignatius Press, 2006)

_____ . *Tradition: Concept and Claim* (Wilmington: ISI Books, 2008).

_____ . *The Silence of St Thomas: Three Essays* (South Bend: St Augustine's Press, 1999)

Servais Pinckaers OP, *Morality: The Catholic View* (South Bend: St Augustine's Press, 2001). This book was designed for teachers; it is based on the same author's important treatise *The Sources of Christian Ethics* (Washington: Catholic University of American Press, 1995)

Plato, *Plato: Complete Works*, ed. John M Cooper (Indianapolis: Hackett, 1997)

Plotinus, *The Enneads*, trans. Stephen MacKenna (London: Faber & Faber, 1956)

Joseph Ratzinger Pope Benedict XVI, *Jesus of Nazareth: From the Baptism in the Jordan to the Transfiguration* (London: Bloomsbury, 2007)

_____ . 'Conscience and Truth,' *Communio* 37 (Fall 2010), 529–38

Giovanni Reale, *Toward a New Interpretation of Plato* (Washington, DC: Catholic University of America Press, 1997)

William Riordan, *Divine Light: The Theology of Denys the Areopagite* (San Francisco: Ignatius Press, 2008)

Jonathan Sacks, *The Dignity of Difference: How to Avoid the Clash of Civilizations* (London: Continuum, 2002)

John Saward, *The Way of the Lamb: The Spirit of Childhood and the End of the Age* (Edinburgh: T&T Clark, 1999)

Dorothy L. Sayers, 'The Lost Tools of Learning,' in *A Matter of Eternity: Selections from the Writings of Dorothy L. Sayers*, ed. Rosamond Kent Sprague (Grand Rapids: Eerdmans, 1973)

D. C. Schindler, *Hans Urs von Balthasar and the Dramatic Structure of Truth: A Philosophical Investigation* (NY: Fordham Univ. Press, 2004)

_____ . 'Metaphysics Within the Limits of Phenomenology: Balthasar and Husserl on the Nature of the Philosophical Act,' *Teología y Vida*, vol. L (2009), 243–58

_____ . 'Truth and the Christian Imagination,' *Communio*, 33 (Winter 2006), 521–39

Bibliography

———. *Ordering Love: Liberal Societies and the Memory of God* (Grand Rapids: Eerdmans, 2011)

E. F. Schumacher, *A Guide for the Perplexed* (London: Jonathan Cape, 1977)

Kenneth L. Schmitz, *At the Center of the Human Drama: The Philosophical Anthropology of Karol Wojtyla/Pope John Paul II* (Washington: Catholic University of America Press, 1993)

———. *The Recovery of Wonder: The New Freedom and the Asceticism of Power* (McGill-Queen's University Press, 2005)

Heinz Schurmann, Joseph Raztinger, Hans Urs von Balthasar, *Principles of Christian Morality* (San Francisco: Ignatius Press, 1986)

Josef Seifert, *Back to Things in Themselves: A Phenomenological Foundation for Classical Realism* (London: Routledge & Kegan Paul, 1987). See also the summary article by Prof. Seifert, 'The Significance of Husserl's Logical Investigations for Realist Phenomenology,' online at www.uc.cl/iapuc/pdf/husserl.pdf

John Senior, *The Restoration of Christian Culture* (San Francisco: Ignatius Press, 1983)

F. J. Sheed, *Ground Plan for Catholic Reading with a Note on Reading and Education* (London: Sheed & Ward, N.D.)

Robert Slesinski, *Pavel Florensky: A Metaphysics of Love* (Crestwood: St Vladimir's Seminary Press, 1984)

C. John Sommerville, *The Rise and Fall of Childhood* (NY: Vintage, 1982)

George Steiner, *Real Presences* (London: Faber & Faber, 1989)

J. R. R. Tolkien, *The Lord of the Rings* (London: George Allen & Unwin, 1969)

———. *Poems and Stories* (London: George Allen & Unwin, 1980)

———. *Sauron Defeated*, The History of Middle-Earth vol. 9, edited by Christopher Tolkien (London: HarperCollins, 1993)

Thomas Traherne, *Centuries* (Oxford: Clarendon Press, 1960)

Kevin Vost, *Memorize the Faith (and Most Anything Else) Using the Methods of the Great Catholic Medieval Memory Masters* (Manchester: Sophia Institute Press, 2006)

E. I. Watkin, *A Philosophy of Form* (London and NY: Sheed & Ward, 1950)

Simone Weil, 'Reflections on the Right Use of School Studies with a View to the Love of God,' in *The Simone Weil Reader*, ed. George A. Panichas (NY: David McKay Co., 1977)

Maureen Wittmann and Rachel Mackson (eds), *The Catholic Homeschool Companion* (Manchester: Sophia Institute Press, 2005)

Karol Wojtyla, *The Acting Person*, trans. Andrezej Potocki, ed. Anna-Teresa Tymieniecka (Netherlands: Reidel, 1979)

Francis Yates, *The Art of Memory* (London: Routledge & Kegan Paul, 1974)

Michael C. Zwaagstra, Rodney A. Clifton, and John C. Long, *What's Wrong with Our Schools and How We can Fix Them* (NY: Rowman & Littlefield, 2010)

SOME WEB RESOURCES

Author's education blog: *http://beauty-in-education.blogspot.com*
The Circe Institute: *www.circeinstitute.org*
Institute for Catholic Liberal Education: *www.catholicliberaleduca-tion.org*

Index of Names

Beauty in the Word
Stratford Caldecott

What is a good education? What is it for? To answer these questions, Stratford Caldecott shines a fresh light on the three arts of language, in a marvelous recasting of the Trivium whereby Grammar, Dialectic, and Rhetoric are explored as Remembering, Thinking, and Communicating. These are the foundational steps every student must take towards conversion of heart and mind, so that a Catholic Faith can be lived out in unabashed pursuit of the True, the Good, and the Beautiful. *Beauty in the Word* is a unique contribution to bringing these bountiful aspects of the Real back to the center of learning, where they rightfully belong. If your concern is for the true meaning of education for your children, here is the place to begin.

"*Beauty in the Word* is the fruit of a lifetime's thinking about the relation between faith and life. Those responsible for new initiatives in Catholic schooling have a chance to recreate the inner spirit of education and not just its outer frame. They will not easily find a programme more inspirational than the one presented here."
—Aidan Nichols, O.P., author of *Redeeming Beauty*

"Stratford Caldecott's words about beauty are themselves beautiful, and also wise, learned and also arresting. He offers a rare combination of intelligence and profound vision, yet combines this with accessibility and luminous transparency."
—Catherine Pickstock, University of Cambridge

"C.S. Lewis envisioned modern education as the irrigation of deserts. Caldecott here brings nourishing water to the cry of the modern imagination: 'I thirst'. Drink deeply, from a book brim-full with the living water capable of transforming our educational practices."
—Cyrus P. Olsen III, University of Scranton

"In this insightful book, Stratford Caldecott has presented a way to understand education in a sense that includes philosophy, theology, the arts, literature, the studies of beauty and truth and what is good. It is a rare book that understands the unity of knowledge and what we want to know. This is one of those rare books."
—James V. Schall, S.J., Georgetown University

STRATFORD CALDECOTT is an editor of the English edition of *Magnificat*, and editor of *Second Spring* and *Humanum*. His books include *The Seven Sacraments: Entering the Mysteries of God* (Crossroad, 2006), and *Beauty for Truth's Sake: On the Re-enchantment of Education* (Brazos, 2009). He lives in Oxford.

Angelico Press

ISBN 978-1-62138-004-7

90000

9 781621 380047